# Day by Day

## with Vance Havner

# *Day by Day*

## with Vance Havner

## 366 Devotions

**BAKER BOOK HOUSE**
Grand Rapids, Michigan 49506

Paperback edition issued by
Baker Book House
with permission of copyright owner

ISBN: 0-8010-4279-8

Library of Congress Catalog Card Number: 54-5430

Printed in the United States of America

## JANUARY 1

### THIS IS THE DAY!

*This is the day which the Lord hath made; we will re-joice and be glad in it.* PSALM 118:24.

THE PSALMIST DOES not mean some special day or holiday nor must we limit this to Sunday or some rare occasion. *Any day* and *every day* is the day which the Lord hath made. Therefore *any day* and *every day* is the day in which to rejoice and be glad. All days are not alike. Some days are more troublesome than others. But the most troublesome may be the most triumphant.

New Year's Day has a bad reputation because it is the birthday of so many resolutions that die in infancy! It is not the day that is so important but the God who made it. Any day is somebody's birthday, and every day really begins a new year. The God who made them all is the Great I Am and lives in a timeless Now. Any day you can begin a new life in Him. "Behold, *now* is the accepted time; behold, *now* is the day of salvation" (II Cor. 6:2).

And every day you can know Him better, for He is "the same *today*" (Heb. 13:8).

## JANUARY 2

### PAUL'S CALENDAR

*I know whom I have believed, and am persuaded that he is able to keep that which I have committed unto him against that day.* II TIMOTHY 1:12.

SOMEONE HAS SAID that Paul's calendar had only two days, "today" and "that day." The man who is ready for *that day*

5

is ready for *any day*. But we need to wear our spiritual bifocals and see both days. Some of the saints are near-sighted.
Some are far-sighted. Paul may have had trouble with his
physical eyes, but he had no spiritual astigmatism. He had
good bifocals; he saw the near and the far.

Do not busy yourself *today* with "wood, hay, stubble,"
and fail to build with "gold, silver, precious stones" against
*that day*. For "*the day* shall declare it," and some lives will
go up in smoke!

On the other hand, do not so contemplate eternity that
you waste today. Some people think they are Mystics when
they are only Mistakes!

"*Today* if ye will hear his voice" (Heb. 4:7).

## JANUARY 3

### HOW TO KEEP FRESH

*We preach not ourselves but Christ Jesus the Lord.*
II CORINTHIANS 4:5.

MAKE JESUS CHRIST your theme! I have seen preachers
espouse causes and champion movements, and when the
cause died and the movement collapsed, the preacher
vanished too. But the man who glories in Christ never grows
stale. Jesus Christ is perennial and he who makes his boast
in Him stays forever fresh. He shall bring forth his fruit in
his season, his leaf also shall not wither, and whatsoever he
doeth shall prosper.

How long it takes us to learn that the issue is simply Jesus! We read books and feel that the magic word is sure to
appear on the next page, but it doesn't. We read biography,
but we cannot live on second-hand experience. We try to
work up visions and ecstasies of our own, but even if we
succeed the glory fades. At last we arrive where we should
have started, to learn that

6

Once it was the blessing;
Now it is the Lord.

It is all Jesus. Why not start at center and work out instead of starting on the circumference and working in? "By him all things consist." Stand at the Hub and all the spokes are yours!

## JANUARY 4

### "THEM TWAIN"

*Not every one that saith unto me, Lord, Lord, shall enter into the kingdom of heaven; but he that doeth the will of my Father which is in heaven.* MATTHEW 7:21.

WE ARE CONSTANTLY seeing living examples of "them twain," the two sons in our Saviour's parable (Mt. 21:28–32). One said, "I will not," but later went. The other said, "I go, Sir," but never went. We have seen some stubborn cases surprise everybody and become obedient servants. Alas, we have seen some walk down church aisles and make a fine show of consecration who never show up in the vineyard. They hear the Word and anon with joy receive it but have no root in themselves and are soon offended.

I am not too elated over your youngster with a chestful of medals and a head full of memory verses. He may volunteer for foreign missions, give a ringing testimony—and never show up in the vineyard. Nor am I too depressed over your headstrong chap who stands adamant while others yield. Young Saul did that for a while.

I am not discrediting the medals, the memory verses and the testimony on the one hand, nor minimizing stubbornness on the other. But the final test of "them twain" in our Saviour's story, as well as in the text for the day, is not saying "Lord, Lord," but doing the Father's will.

7

# JANUARY 5

## DO WHAT YOU CAN

*She hath done what she could.* MARK 14:8.

HE HAD FOUND a little box in the attic. With his crayons he had tried to make it more presentable. Inside he had placed a cut-out Santa Claus and a larger Santa of his own drawing. He had scrawled "Season's Greetings" for a touch of dignity. Then he had wrapped it in a manner all his own, with plenty of seals all over and a big yellow ribbon tied all around.

It wouldn't bring much on sale, but no one could buy it from me, because it was the expression of a little boy's love and, oh, so welcome!

He had done what he could. Which sets me thinking of the woman who anointed Jesus. "She hath done what she could." Do not let not being able to do it better keep you from doing what you can. Bring to the Saviour such as you have, the best you have, all you have. He will receive it. It may seem a poor little thing to others, but if it is the love gift of your heart, it will be precious in His sight.

Do what you can.


# JANUARY 6

## CHRIST OR ANTICHRIST

*He that is not with me is against me; and he that gathereth not with me scattereth abroad.* MATTHEW 12:30.

AFTER ALL IS said and done, the real issue today, as always, is Christ or Antichrist. We try to move the focal point elsewhere, but here is where the battle rages. And if Christ is the issue, then for us the supreme matter is (1) to become a Christian; (2) to become a better Christian daily; (3) to help other Christians to be better Christians, and (4) to help those who are not Christians to become Christians. We gather with Him, or we scatter abroad.

This is our real "program," faith in Christ, fellowship with Christ, faithfulness to Christ, fruitfulness for Christ. It simplifies life to one thing, just to be a Christian, a believer in Christ, a follower of Christ, a witness of Christ.

Anything less is not enough. Anything more is too much. "With me"—there is our position; "gathering"—there is our practice. "Follow me and I will make you fishers of men." Following and fishing!

Are you Christian or Antichristian?

## JANUARY 7

### COME FOR YOURSELF

*Him that cometh unto me I will in no wise cast out.*
JOHN 6:37.

VARIOUS "RULES" AND "steps" have been proposed for seekers after salvation, the filling of the Spirit, guidance and other experiences of the Christian life. Sometimes they confuse more than they clarify. No two experiences are alike. We tend to make a norm of our own and force it upon others. Coming to Jesus is a personal matter, not a dry business procedure. Nobody ever fell in love by reading books on how to fall in love. We meet someone, associate with someone, and either fall in love or not fall in love. There are, indeed, certain conditions that must be met in a personal

9

knowledge of Christ, but it is more like falling in love than a cold business deal. There is a sense of need, a drawing near, a fellowship that ripens with the years. The expressions and manifestations vary with different types and temperaments. Do not try to imitate a made-to-order experience handed down from someone else. He invites you to come as you are and know Him for yourself.

## REPORT OR REALITY?

*But him they saw not.* LUKE 24:24.

THE EMMAUS DISCIPLES had the testimony of the women, the angels and other disciples, but, like these other disciples, they had not seen the risen Lord Himself to know Him. Something had happened. Jesus was not in the grave. But they had not seen Him.

There is a lot of talk about the ressurection that gets no farther than that. Something happened. The grave is empty. But there is lacking the vibrant witness, "We have seen the Lord!"

Much is said about the return of Christ that lacks the warmth of His person. We discuss the program of events, what is going to happen, "but him we see not."

That goes for all the great truths about Him. We tell what others have said. We discuss the matter. But Him we see not. Our eyes are holden. A few minutes later these Emmaus disciples were not like the same persons. They had a glowing testimony, and as they related it He appeared again! His resurrection was no longer a Report but a Reality!

10

## JANUARY 9

### THAT ALL MAY KNOW

*The Lord knoweth them that are his.* II TIMOTHY 2:19.
*We know that we are of God.* I JOHN 5:19.
*By this shall all men know that ye are my disciples, if
ye have love one to another.* JOHN 13:35.

GOD KNOWS HIS own. It is well that He does, for sometimes
it would be difficult for us to determine who are His!
Heaven will surprise us both ways.

We can know that we are His. The little book of First
John is full of "know-so" evidence, to say nothing of plenty
more elsewhere.

And others know by the badge of love. Not tongues nor
faith nor prophecy nor knowledge nor martyrdom nor
philanthropy, but love is the Christian's mark of distinction.
How we cultivate all the others and fail here!

All may know that we are His. God knows, we know,
others may know. It is a "Know-so" faith.

## JANUARY 10

### HIS PLACE FOR YOU

*But all these worketh that one and the selfsame Spirit,
dividing to every man severally as he will.* I CORIN-
THIANS 12:11.

WHEN A FAMOUS preacher arises, swaying the crowds, one
by-product is that some of his contemporaries begin to
imagine that they must be out of God's will or not filled with
the Spirit because they are not achieving similar results.
But God is sovereign. He chooses men for special tasks, and
if one hits the headlines, that is no reflection on the host of
unknowns. The Spirit divideth severally as He will. A coun-

11

try preacher ministering to two hundred people may be as Spirit-filled to his capacity as was Moody.

Moody had around him many lesser lights who helped him in his work, who filled their orbits as well as he filled his. And what would the "big" preacher do without the help of the "small fry"?

Seek neither more nor less than God's will for you. Do not compare yourself with men above or below you in station, lest you be depressed or exalted.

Simply find His place for you and happily serve Him there. Anywhere He puts you is a "large place"!

## JANUARY 11

### SAND OR SEED

*Faith as a grain of mustard seed.* MATTHEW 17:20.

IF YOU WOULD develop a living faith, not like a grain of sand but like a grain of seed, do not read too many books on faith. One dear brother will tell you that you must agonize and strive to enter, while another would have you "take it by faith." Both are right: you must mean business and be in dead earnest, but beyond that you must, like Hudson Taylor, quit working at your faith and rest in the Faithful One.

Books on faith are colored by the author's temperament, theology, experience, style of expression. You can become more concerned about the quantity and quality of your faith than about its object. You never will get your experience to suit you. You will never pray just as you want to, or feel or preach or live just as you want to. Perfection is found only in Him.

Real faith stops studying itself and is occupied with Him. Quit digging in the ashes of your poor heart for satisfaction. Consider Him—not your faith—"lest ye be weary and faint in your minds."

12

## "THE GOOD OLD DAYS"

*Where is the Lord God of Elijah?* II KINGS 2:14.

ELISHA DID NOT ask for the return of Elijah or sigh for the good old days of Elijah. Some of us are like Saul trying to call up departed Samuels. "What would Moody do today? Oh, for the times we used to have!"

A subscriber wrote to a magazine editor, "Your magazine is not as good as it used to be." The editor replied, "It never has been." The times have never been as good as they used to be! The Early Church, fresh from Pentecost, had barely started, when "there arose a murmuring." Look at Corinth! Don't forget Ananias and Sapphira, the Galatians and Colossians, Euodia and Syntyche, the plight of Ephesus, Sardis, Laodicea. It has always been so, yet God has carried on.

Looking back to the good old days is not the way out. Looking up to the God of All the Days is.

Elijah goes, but "thou, O Lord, remainest."

## STOPPING SHORT OF GOD

*O God, thou art my God; early will I seek thee: my soul thirsteth for thee, my flesh longeth for thee in a dry and thirsty land, where no water is.* PSALM 63:1.

ANY SPIRITUAL EXERCISE that stops short of God Himself stops far too short. We can become taken up with the means and forget the end. Our Bible reading may bring us profit and we may lay down the Book with a comfortable sense of duty well performed, but does the heart say, "Beyond the sacred page, I seek Thee, Lord"? Prayer is but a means to an end: we may get a secret satisfaction out of praying that makes prayer only an end in itself. "Early will I seek *thee*" —that is true prayer. "Now *thee* alone I seek, give what is best." Faith has no value save as it links us with God. Yet we often become taken up with our faith and miss God entirely.

Feelings, experiences, meditation, reading, church attendance, with all these we may stop short of God, finding some satisfaction but letting the good rob us of the best— Himself. The Psalmist said, "My soul thirsteth . . . my flesh longeth for thee." Only God can meet the need of the whole man.

## JANUARY 14

### "COME AND DRINK"

*My soul thirsteth.* PSALM 63:1.
*If any man thirst* . . . JOHN 7:37.

"BUT HOW CAN my thirsting soul find God? He is too abstract, I can form no mental picture of Him. How can I drink of the Living Water?"

That is why Jesus came. In Him the Word became flesh. No man comes to the Father but by Him, and whosoever comes to Him will in no wise be cast out.

"If any man thirst, let Him come unto me and drink. He that believeth on me, from within him shall flow rivers of living water." Thirsting, coming, drinking, believing, overflowing—the thirsting soul comes and receives and believes that it has received (Mk. 11:24). The overflowing is a natural—a supernatural—consequence—"shall flow."

A little tenement child in a hospital, presented with a large glass of cool, rich milk, asked hesitantly, "How deep may I drink?" Drink deeply of the Living Water!

"Ho, every one that thirsteth, come ye to the waters."

14

## JANUARY 15

### FRUIT OF THE LAND

*How long are ye slack to possess the land which the Lord God of your fathers giveth you?* JOSHUA 18:3.

WE OUGHT NOT stand on Jordan's stormy banks casting a wishful eye to Canaan's fair and happy land, where our possessions lie. "Dwelling in Beulah Land" is possible here and now. Living in Canaan may be a *fact* today.

It is also a *fight*, the fight of faith, as we follow our Joshua, the Captain of our salvation and "possess our possessions."

And there will be *fruit*. "This is the fruit of it," said the spies (Num. 13:27). "The fruit of the Spirit" it is today (Gal. 5:22, 23). Alas, so many are still in the wilderness, longing for garlic instead of grace, melons instead of manna!

The best advertisement of the land is the fruit of it. Where are your milk and honey? Men will believe the *fact* when from the *fight* you bring the *fruit*.

## JANUARY 16

### REVIVAL—OR ELSE

*Thou hast left thy first love.* REVELATION 2:4.

IN THE COURSE of history, Christianity periodically clutters up with its own projects and paraphernalia. Then God raises up a new fellowship of fresh Christians somewhere, all aglow in simple faith and obedience. Sometimes this happens in a local church, either when the old crowd has a revival or there is a blood transfusion of new converts.

In individual experience we tend to get away from our first love, not always into false doctrine or worldly living,

15

but, like the saints at Ephesus, while still orthodox and busy at church work.

Happy is the man who can go deeply into profound doctrine or multiplied activities and yet not lose the warmth of simple faith and love. How to maintain the glow of our early love for Christ amidst all the complexities of today and not lose the best amongst the good is a major matter. How to delve deeply into the mysteries of God and still be just a simple Christian; how to work hard in involved labors of the church and yet be just a humble believer is a supreme concern.

If you have left your first love, the way back is *Remember, Repent, Repeat*. Our Lord offers a grievous alternative . . . *Removal*. It is *Revival*—or else.

## JANUARY 17

### ARE YOU "IN LOVE"?

*Neither cold nor hot.* REVELATION 3:16.

LET US PURSUE further our thought of yesterday. While we cry out against liberalism and loose living, are we not blind to the peril of lukewarmness? What was once a boiling passion for Christ becomes tepid and mild. We sing the same songs, recite the same Scriptures, perchance preach the same sermons as before, but we are like the fountains sometimes seen in public parks with water gushing from mouths that never taste it. We are salt without savour. We traffic in unfelt truth.

> In vain we sing our formal songs,
> In vain we strive to rise;
> Hosannas languish on our tongues
> And our devotion dies.

The church has no greater need today than to fall in love with Jesus all over again. Call it what you will, we need a heart-warming. There is a world of difference between studying books on love and falling in love. We are going through the motions without the motive.

A few Christians desperately in love with Christ mean more than a host of indifferent church members whose Christianity has become just another "big business" of committees and budgets and programs.

## JANUARY 18

### GOD HAS NO GRANDCHILDREN

*To him that knoweth to do good and doeth it not, to him it is sin.* JAMES 4:17.

GIBBON DESCRIBES THE degeneration of Christianity under the Greek scholars of the 10th century, who handled the literature and spoke the language of the spiritual but knew not the life: "They held in their lifeless hands the riches of their fathers without inheriting the spirit which had created and imparted that sacred patrimony. They read; they praised; they compiled; but their languid souls seemed alike incapable of thought and action."

The Pharisees of Jesus' day handled the things of God, read the Scriptures, faithfully kept the letter of the law, were painstakingly separated from sinners. But the publicans and harlots went into the Kingdom before them.

To have grown up in a Christian home and in a church, early fluent in the speech of the Kingdom, familiar with its subjects and observing its practices, yet never a citizen, produces a type of sinner often harder to awaken than the most ignorant heathen. Truth long heard and not acted upon means awful self-deception (James 1:22).

Second generations do not inherit salvation. God has no grandchildren.

17

## JANUARY 19

### INCLUDED IN THE TICKET

*He that spared not his own Son, but delivered him up for us all, how shall he not with him also freely give us all things?* ROMANS 8:32.

IT IS AN old story of the ship passenger who lived on crackers and cheese all the way across the ocean only.to learn that his meals were included in his ticket.

Our salvation includes more than pardon from sin, deliverance from hell and a ticket to heaven. It includes all that we shall need on our journey. Sin has been dealt with in the Son, but Jesus is not only our Saviour, He is our Sustenance and Supply. We are not to subsist on our own crackers and cheese. "All things are yours." Indeed, the supreme thing is that God spared not His own Son but delivered Him up for us all. That is the message of Calvary. But God has also freely given us all things in the gift of His Son. Our assurance, sanctification, peace, joy, wisdom, all that we need for body, mind and spirit to do God's will, a new body at the resurrection, eternal life in heaven, all this is "included in the ticket."

What a "ticket," bought at the purchase price of God's own Son! Throw away your crackers and cheese! You have a right to eat in the Main Dining Room!

### JANUARY 20

### "YES" AND "NO"

*Submit yourselves therefore to God. Resist the devil and he will flee from you.* JAMES 4:7.

A WELL-KNOWN WRITER says that this verse means, "Say, 'Yes,' to God and, 'No,' to the devil. It is useless to try to resist the devil without first submitting to God. The devil is too strong for us. Victory begins with surrender—to God. But, on the other hand, we are to follow submission to God with resisting the devil. "The battle is the Lord's," but we are not machines, we must put our wills on God's side and say, "No," to the enemy. We fight with spiritual weapons, but we still fight, and there is not only passive submission but active resistance.

Some make the mistake of mere submission without a positive stand against the tempter. Others resist without submission, and the devil does not flee. It is a double-barreled admonition. It is a clear-cut call to "Yes" and "No."

"Let your speech be Yea, yea; Nay, nay."

## JANUARY 21
### WHAT KIND OF FAITH?

*According to your faith be it unto you.*
MATTHEW 9:29.

"Do I HAVE the right kind of faith?" Dr. Biederwolf used to say, "If you have any faith at all, you may be sure it is the right kind." Do not waste time taking your faith apart and putting it back together. Do not expect saving faith to be some strange, different kind. You believe in Christ with faith like the faith you use when you trust someone or something else. It is the object that makes the difference.

If you have any uncertainty about the matter, come to a definite decision. Trust Christ now. It may help you to put down the time and place. You must have confidence in the decision and consider it settled. But do not confuse faith in your faith with faith in the Saviour. Faith has no value of its own, it has value only as it connects us with Him.

It is a trick of Satan to get us occupied with examining our faith instead of resting in the Faithful One. Go to Him just as you are as best you know. Him that cometh He will not cast out.

19

## JANUARY 22

### WINE OR VINEGAR?

*Thy word was unto me the joy and rejoicing of mine heart.* JEREMIAH 15:16.

McLAREN SPEAKS OF the "perverse ingenuity . . . of that state of mind in which some manage to distil for themselves a bitter vinegar of self-accusation out of grand words in the Bible that were meant to afford them but the wine of gladness and of consolation."

The Spirit does indeed use the Word to convict the guilty and uneasy conscience, but, on the other hand, the Accuser may so beset us that Scriptures meant to give us assurance may but make us miserable. The devil is the author of a false confidence but he also generates a false diffidence, so that we get vinegar out of what should be wine to our souls.

If you have definitely committed all you are and have to God, do not be afraid to enjoy the wine of the Word. Do not cultivate a perverted taste that distils vinegar instead.

## JANUARY 23

### SECOND ADAM

*For as in Adam all die, even so in Christ shall all be made alive.* I CORINTHIANS 15:22.

WE ARE ALL children of the first Adam. He fell and to this day we suffer the consequences. Sin, disease, death, all the corruptions and frailties of the body, mind and spirit, we inherit from our father, the first man of the earth, earthy.

But God started a new race with His Son from heaven. To as many as receive Him to them gives He power to become the sons of God, even to them that believe on His

20

Name. Read Romans 5 for a glorious picture of the two Adams.

Here is the true superrace of sons of God whose citizenship is in heaven. We still carry the marks of Adam's fall, and our bifocals and bridges and baldness and all our frailties bear witness that we are his offspring. But from the day we believe, we begin a new life which shall discard this shell for a new body at the resurrection. Our New Adam is perfect, and all we need here and hereafter is found in Him. We can reign in life now by Christ Jesus.

## JANUARY 24

### "NOTHING WAVERING"

*But let him ask in faith, nothing wavering.* JAMES 1:6.

THE MAN WHO lacks wisdom is promised it, but he must ask in faith and not be like a wave of the sea, driven with the wind and tossed. Our Lord said we could move mountains if we commanded them to move *and did not doubt in our hearts* (Mk. 11:23). The positive side of that is in the next verse, which says, "What things soever ye desire, when ye pray, believe that ye recveive them, and ye shall have them."

Abraham "staggered not at the promise of God through unbelief; but was strong in faith." There we have the negative and positive again (Rom. 4:20). Some are saved from sin but not from staggering.

"Let him ask in faith, nothing wavering." Positive and negative! Are you walking by faith or wobbling in doubt? "We lie to God in prayer when we do not rely on God after prayer." James is very clear: "Let not that man think he shall receive anything of the Lord."

Asking without believing marks a double-minded man, unstable in all his ways.

21

## JANUARY 25

### "BUT IF NOT . . ."

*Our God is able to deliver us . . . But if not . . .*
DANIEL 3:17, 18.

THE HEBREW CHILDREN did not doubt that God could save them from the furnace, but if He did not they would be faithful, anyway. It is well to be prepared for the "if nots." God is always able, but sometimes it is not His will to deliver us from the fiery furnace. But He will save us *in* the furnace. He does not always spare us trouble, but He does succour us *in* trouble.

If you are facing a furnace, make provision for the "if not." If you are not healed, if the dear one is taken, if that friend fails you, be faithful, anyway. "Though he slay me, yet will I trust him." If things do not turn out the way you had hoped and prayed they would, do not bow to Nebuchadnezzar's image of doubt or fear or discouragement. That is what the devil wants, as when he put Job in his furnace.

"God can do it, but if He doesn't, He is still my God. I will bow to no idol." . . . Blessed are the saints of the If Nots!

## JANUARY 26

### "AND OTHERS"

*And others were tortured, . . .* HEBREWS 11:35

THIS "WESTMINSTER ABBEY of the Bible" rises through a glorious galaxy of faith-heroes, Abel, Enoch, Noah, Abraham, and many more, until it reaches a pinnacle in a summary of those who wrought righteousness, subdued kingdoms, obtained promises, stopped the mouths of lions, quenched the violence of fire, escaped the edge of the sword, out of weakness were made strong, waxed valiant in fight, turned to flight the armies of the aliens, of women who received their dead raised to life again.

But not all fare that way. Suddenly the verse changes gears: "And others were tortured, mocked, scourged, put in bonds and imprisonment, were stoned, sawn asunder, tempted, slain with the sword, wandered, being destitute."

Faith is not a sure road to the headlines, success, earthly victories, and deliverance from harm and danger. Some move grandly through in that first procession—and who wouldn't like to be in that crowd? But there are others for whom things go the other way.

One thing they all had in common: "And these all, *having obtained a good report through faith . . .*" We can do that, no matter which procession we are in!

## JANUARY 27

### SUBTILTY AND SIMPLICITY

*But I fear, lest by any means, as the serpent beguiled Eve through his* subtilty, *so your minds should be corrupted from the simplicity that is in Christ.* II CORINTHIANS 11:3.

Strictly speaking, what is in mind here is the simplicity of our faith in Christ rather than the simplicity of the Gospel, but we need not stop there. What stands out most is the contrast between subtilty and simplicity. Satan deals in subtilties. Our Lord deals in simplicities. There is sublimity aplenty but the sublimity is revealed to the simple, kept from the wise and prudent and revealed unto babes. We have let our minds be corrupted by Satan's subtilties away from the Saviour's simplicities. Beware of any teaching, any movement that is sneaking and insidious. The truth is frank and honest and aboveboard. Satan's subtilties bear the mark of the serpent—"the snake in the grass." Our Lord stood in the public place and invited men to Him. The Early Church came out in the open. Paul said, "This thing was not done in a corner."

It is part of Satan's program to make our faith and practice complicated and involved. Now and then we need a rediscovery of the simplicity that is both in and toward Christ, in Him and in our faith in Him.

## JANUARY 28

### "IF ANY MAN WILL . . ."

*If any man will do his will, he shall know of the doctrine, whether it be of God, or whether I speak of myself.* JOHN 7:17.

THE BATTLE IS fought in the citadel of the will. We have intelligence, emotions, and will. We may not be able to understand with the intelligence or feel with the emotions as we would like, but we can take a stand in the will and be true to God, however all else may clamor.

Do not yield to confusion. Are you a man or a mob? Too many today do not have themselves in order and under command. Many a man is not a personality, he is a panic!

Of course, our poor wills, left unaided, are but cotton strings. But when we will the will of God He begins to work in us both to will and do of his good pleasure (Phil. 2:13). We submit to His will: "Thy will be done." Then we assert His will: "Thy will be done!" It is both passive and active. "Thy will be done" is not mere resignation to the inevitable, it is affirmation of the invincible. However little the intelligence may understand or emotion feel, we take our stand in the will yielded to His will.

# JANUARY 29

## THE SECRET INGREDIENT

*The secret of the Lord is with them that fear him.*
PSALM 25:14.

EVERYTHING HAS THAT mysterious "something" nowadays, whether washing powder or gasoline or vitamin pills or shaving cream or tooth paste—everything has that new added element that no other brand has. This magic X has a wonderful unpronounceable name not yet in any dictionary. We smile, but thousands of gullible mortals will buy truckloads of the hokum and find it no better than something else they fell for months ago.

But there is a secret ingredient that makes one brand of people different from all others. It is not some new religious fad or ism, although these too shout their magic formulas today. There are among us here and there those who have a deep inner peace and joy, "who ply their daily task with busier feet because their secret souls a holier strain repeat."

No double-jointed theological jawbreaker is needed to name that secret ingredient. It is simply the grace of God, peace with God, and the peace of God in the trustful and obedient heart. "His secret is with the righteous" (Prov. 3:32).


# JANUARY 30

## "TAKE IT EASY"

*I will say to my soul, Soul, . . . take thine ease.*
LUKE 12:19.

THE RICH FOOL was no fool as a farmer, he was a success. He was religious because he talked to his soul. So many

25

seem not to know they have souls! But his clock was too slow. He said, "Many years," but God said, "This night."

He was never a bigger fool than when he told his soul to take it easy. No man ought ever tell his soul that. Too many souls are taking it easy. I do not believe in soul-sleeping after death, but plenty of souls are sleeping now.

The rich fool gave his soul the wrong advice. He put it on vacation. God does not give the soul a vacation, He gives it a vocation.

"Take it easy" is a familiar parting word nowadays which nobody heeds by relaxing and living sensibly in this age of stomach ulcers and aspirin tablets. But it is no proper word for our souls. Rather, "Awake, my soul, stretch every nerve and press with vigor on," ought to be the theme song of stupefied saints at ease in Zion. And while the sinner orders his soul to take it easy he may gain the world but he loses his soul. He is forever damned because he took it easy and neglected so great salvation.

## JANUARY 31

### HAVE YOU A RESERVATION?

*I go to prepare a place for you.* JOHN 14:2.
*An inheritance incorruptible and undefiled and that fadeth not away, reserved in heaven for you.* I PETER 1:4.

How GOOD IT is when the weary traveler can walk up to the hotel desk and find a room ready and waiting, while others may ask in vain—and all because his name is on the book; he made a reservation.

We cannot walk up to the gate of heaven after death and obtain a dwelling-place merely by asking for it. Our abiding place up there is secured in advance while we are down here. Our Saviour has gone to prepare a place, but there are places only for those who make reservations. Is your name in the book?

Many will come in that day and make various claims, but he will say, "Depart, I never knew you." The dying thief made a reservation: "Remember me." Reservations are made, not on the basis of our merit, but on His merit and our simple faith in Him.

Have you a reservation?

## FEBRUARY 1

### SAVIOUR OR SONG?

*Behold, God is my salvation; I will trust, and not be afraid: for the Lord Jehovah is my strength and my song; he also is become my salvation.* ISAIAH 12:2.

A WELL-KNOWN PASTOR tells of a soloist who sang with real artistry a great Gospel song one Sunday morning. By musical standards it was flawless, but the minister detected a lack of "heart," although there was plenty of art. At the door he asked the singer, "Was that song real to you or was it just a song?" She flushed, but she was honest, and she finally replied, "Pastor, I'm afraid it was just a song."

We should have both, a Saviour and a song. The Lord Jehovah is our salvation, our strength and our song. When He lifts us out of the miry clay and puts our feet on the Rock, He also puts a song in our mouth. But nothing is so hollow as singing something we know nothing about. A lot of that goes on in churches on Sunday mornings, it is to be feared, and no matter how much of "art" there is, it will not make up for lack of "heart."

Is the Lord your salvation and strength or is He "just a song"?

27

## FEBRUARY 2

### FROM HEARING TO SEEING

*I have heard of thee by the hearing of the ear; but now mine eye seeth thee.* JOB 42:5.

JOB WAS A good man already. He feared God and eschewed evil, and God called him "my servant Job" and said of him, "There is none like him in the earth." Job had heard and had believed. That is good enough to start with. "Faith cometh by hearing and hearing by the word of God." Moreover, Job had lived an exemplary life.

But, like many who have come that far, he needed to *see* God, not in a vision or manifestation to the senses but in a personal, overwhelming, humbling, pride-shattering consciousness of the very presence of God Himself.

Through the ages, such an experience, though wide and diverse in its patterns, has marked the men God has used most. Too many have heard and believed and lived but have not seen. God brings us to where we can say, *"But now mine eye seeth thee!"*

## FEBRUARY 3

### SANCTIFIED FOR OTHERS

*For their sakes I sanctify myself.* JOHN 17:19.

THERE IS A sense in which we, too, must sanctify ourselves for the sake of others. We live in a sin-sick world infested and infected by the microbes of evil. We live in a satanic world order, and as the physician seeks to save the patient while he fights the disease we must love the souls of men but contend with the sinful powers that beset them. Surgeons and nurses must keep fit and clean, and so must we who bear the vessels of the Lord. We must keep strong by the food of the Word, by resting in the Lord, by exercising unto godliness. If we develop points of infection they must be dealt with. Any habit or interest that lowers our resistance to evil must be abandoned. The offending eye or hand must be plucked out or cut off, for sometimes spiritual surgery is indicated. "Habits of life though harmless they seem" must be dropped if they get between the soul and the Saviour so that His blessed face is not seen.

For God's sake, for the sake of others, for our own sakes, let us sanctify ourselves.

## FEBRUARY 4

### HIMSELF

*By him all things consist.* COLOSSIANS 1:17.

THE SUPREME EXPERIENCE is to get past all lesser experiences to Christ Himself. Most of us stop short of the Giver because we are forever seeking this or that gift. Many a saint can testify to years of being occupied with this doctrine and that, this blessing and that, but coming one day into the larger place of resting in the Lord Himself, finding in Him their reward, their portion. Anything short of that is fractional, immature, incomplete. We are complete in Him, not in any experience or favorite doctrine. Here is the experience that excels all experiences because it includes them all. The whole is greater than any of the parts.

"Getting through to God" is not a strange emotional experience—although it may indeed move the emotions— but simply arriving at the blessed point where we rest in the Blesser and not in a lesser "blessing." Then, whatever we may lose, we have Him, and in Him we have everything. All things are ours, and we are Christ's and Christ is God's.

## TAKE HOLD OF GOD!

*There is none that stirreth up himself to take hold of thee.* ISAIAH 64:7.

THE PROPHET IS not lamenting that there is none that stirreth up himself. There have never been more "rousements" in our religious life than today. We whip our jaded nerves into a St. Vitus's dance but it is an end in itself; we do not get through to God. The way out of a spiritual stupor is not by getting into a stew. The stirring up of ourselves is a means to an end, to take hold of God. We must rouse ourselves to employ the means of grace, draw nigh to God that He may draw nigh to us.

We must stir up the gift of God. Like sugar in the lemonade, it may be there but it needs to be set in motion. The ashes need to be scraped off the coals in our hearts and the fire rekindled.

A lot of our religious bustle today does not take hold of God. We get excited and strike in all directions and keep the Lord busy putting back ears we lop off in our misdirected zeal, like Peter at the Saviour's arrest. It is not merely stepping up our activities nor is it an emotional binge; it is arousing ourselves to employ the means God has provided, the Word, prayer, and all other ways of laying hold of Him.

## FEBRUARY 6

### THE TECHNIQUE OF THE TOWEL

*If I then, your Lord and Master, have washed your feet; ye also ought to wash one another's feet.* JOHN 13:14.

OUR LORD STEPS from magnificence to meniality: "Jesus knowing that the Father had given all things into his hands

. . . began to wash the disciples' feet." From sublimity to service!

In the early days of Communism one leader wanted to admit all who accepted the theory and purposes of the movement. Lenin insisted that only those who were so devoted as to be willing to do the most menial tasks be received. "Fewer but better" was his motto. He said, "Give me one hundred fanatics rather than a thousand indifferent followers."

"The children of this world are in their generation wiser than the children of light." Considering how we have to coax and beg church members to do a few things for our Lord, we can easily see how we are loaded down with excess baggage, nominal disciples who agree in theory but have never learned our Saviour's technique of the towel.

The average church member would do well to look in his concordance and see how many columns it takes to list all the "serve," "servant," "service" references. We come to church to sit but will not go out to serve.

## FEBRUARY 7

### WHAT LACK I YET?

*What lack I yet?* MATTHEW 19:20.

THE RICH YOUNG ruler had morals, manners and money. He would be welcomed readily into many churches today, with no questions asked. He would make a good "joiner," but he would be a poor disciple.

Salvation is free but discipleship costs everything. Somehow, we have utterly lost sight of our Saviour's drastic and often severe challenges to prospective disciples. Letting the dead bury the dead, denying self, hating loved ones, putting the hand to the plow—He used terms that demanded absolute obedience and unquestionable loyalty. Today we have tempered all this down and removed its sharp edge and have gathered a host of indifferent "joiners'" who have not the faintest idea of what it means to "sell out" for Christ.

Jesus lost this prospect. The young man went away. Why didn't our Lord take him on milder terms and later lead him into complete surrender? That is our technique today, but Jesus was out for disciples, not "joiners."

"What lack I yet?" Here is the painful lack in our churches, because it is the lack of so many of their members.

## FEBRUARY 8

### "GET" OR "GIVE"?

*Then answered Peter and said unto him, Behold, we have forsaken all, and followed thee;* what shall we have therefore? MATTHEW 19:27.
*Then Peter said, Silver and gold have I none;* but such as I have give I thee: *in the name of Jesus Christ of Nazareth rise up and walk.* ACTS 3:6.

A LOT OF water had run under the bridge in Peter's experience between these verses. Too many disciples are out for what they can get instead of what they can give. "What do I get out of church, what is there in the Christian life for me?" Church members too often expect service and never think of giving it.

Peter had no money to offer but he performed a miracle. The church today no longer says, "Silver and gold have I none," but neither can she say, "Rise and walk." Men, money, movements, there are aplenty but few miracles. And there will be none until the Getters become Givers.

Have you moved from "What do I get?" to "What can I give?"

## GET THROUGH TO JESUS!

*If any man thirst, let him come unto me, and drink.*
JOHN 7:37.

SOME STOP TOO soon in their quest for a satisfying experience of the Lord. They get this blessing or that and settle down there and make their blessing an end in itself and a yardstick by which they measure everybody else. The part becomes greater than the whole. They major on the gift instead of on the Giver. Others experience no "blessing" at all, give up and resign themselves to a dry faith, and plod along through dull and mediocre years.

Others go too far. They run past the Lord into delusions and excesses and fall into snares of demonism. Pitiful cases they are, starting out honestly and earnestly, but not guided by the Word.

Jesus simply invites us to Himself, whether for rest (Mt. 11:28) or for the Spirit's fulness (Jno. 7:37), and guarantees that if we come He will not cast us out (Jno. 6:37). It is not difficult to get to Jesus if we really want to come. And anyone who gets through to Him will be all right. "All the fitness He requireth is to feel your need of Him."

## HIS BLOOD AND HIS BIDDING

*Christ died for our sins.* I CORINTHIANS 15:3
*Come unto me.* MATTHEW 11:28.

Just as I am, without one plea
But that thy blood was shed for me,
And that Thou bid'st me come to Thee,
O Lamb of God, I come, I come.

WE DO NOT come on the ground of His teaching, His character, His life, but rather on the ground of His death.

The problem of our sin was not taken care of until Calvary. There is a salvation offered today on the ground of Christ the Example, Christ the Teacher, Christ the Ideal, but the sinner does not come on the plea that "Thy life was lived for me," or "Thy example was revealed for me." Christ's life and example and teaching have their place and a great and glorious place it is, but I come in my sins because His blood was shed for me.

And then *His Bidding*. He invited me. He bids me come, just as I am. I don't have to dress up. He will dress me up after I come. My righteousnesses—the best I am and can do —are but filthy rags, rags because they do not cover me and filthy because they only defile me.

HIS BLOOD: "But that *Thy blood* was shed for me."

HIS BIDDING: "And that *Thou bid'st* me come to thee."

May your answer be, "O Lamb of God, I come!"


## FEBRUARY 11

### THE WORD OR THE WORLD

*I have given them thy* word; *and the* world *hath hated them because they are not of the world, even as I am not of the world.* JOHN 17:14.

IF YOU STAND on the Word you do not stand in with the world. McLaren says, "The measure of our *discord* with the world is the measure of our *accord* with our Saviour." Our Lord said the world hated Him and would hate us. "If ye were of the world, the world would love its own: but because ye are not of the world, but I have chosen you out of the world, therefore the world hateth you" (John 15:18–19).

"The world knoweth us not, because it knew him not" (I John 3:1). What has happened to all this today? The average church member courts the world's favor and re-joices in being hail-fellow-well-met and shows off the world's prizes and rewards. If to love the world is to be the enemy of God, we have some strange contradictions among us!

What some think is the world becoming more Christian is just Christians becoming more worldly. We can have the *word* or the *world* but not both. There is no concord between Christ and Belial. Read John 17; II Corinthians 6: 14–7:1; James 4:4; I John 2:15–17. We are strangers here. Don't make yourself at home.

## FEBRUARY 12

### TWO LOST WORDS

*All power is given unto me in heaven and in earth. Go ye therefore and teach all nations, baptizing them in the name of the Father, and of the Son, and of the Holy Ghost; teaching them to observe all things whatsoever I have commanded you: and, lo, I am with you alway, even unto the end of the world.* MATTHEW 28:18–20.

HERE IS OUR Saviour's *prerogative*: He claims all power; our Saviour's *program*: discipling, baptizing, teaching; our Saviour's *promise:* to be with us all the days, even to the consummation of the age.

What a set-up! All the world before us, all power behind us, the All-powerful One with us!

In the teaching phase of our Saviour's *program*, we do not read, "teaching them all things whatsoever I have commanded you." Much of our teaching today is just that, the dissemination of information. It says, "teaching them *to observe* . . ." Here are the two lost words of the Great Commission. Throughout the Word of God the accent is on *doing, observing, keeping* the commandments of the Lord. Today we teach them, but we do not teach people to do them. The Word is hid in the head but not in the heart. It is the Word hidden in the heart that keeps from sin. You can have a head full of Scripture and a heart full of sin.

### FEBRUARY 13

### REPROACH AND/OR RICHES

*Esteeming the reproach of Christ greater riches than the treasures in Egypt.* HEBREWS 11:26.

MOSES HAD TO choose one of two kinds of wealth, the reproach of Christ or the treasures of Egypt. He esteemed the first to be the greater riches and so laid up treasure in heaven.

He *chose the imperishable,* "choosing rather to suffer affliction with the people of God than to enjoy the pleasures of sin *for a season.*" He *saw the invisible*: "He endured as seeing him who is invisible"; He did the *impossible*: "By faith they passed through the Red Sea."

Moses got off to a good start in his parentage. This same account tells us (v. 23) that his parents hid him when he was a baby and that "they were not afraid of the king's commandment." We read later that Moses forsook Egypt, "not fearing the wrath of the king." Like parents, like son!

Moses' choice was reproach and/or riches. It is a matter of whether one wants to get rich or be rich. We can be rich

36

in Christ Jesus or perhaps get rich in Egypt, but we cannot do both. It is never "Christ and . . ." It is always "Christ or . . ." We cannot serve God and mammon.

## CHOOSING YOUR ANGEL

*Are they not all ministering spirits, sent forth to minister for them who shall be heirs of salvation?* HEBREWS 1:14.
*Satan himself is transformed into an angel of light.* II CORINTHIANS 11:14.
*Beloved, believe not every spirit, but try the spirits whether they are of God.* I JOHN 4:1.

ANGELS MINISTERED TO Jesus, they minister for the saints, they minister to little children. But Satan goes about as a Mock Angel and does more harm in that pose than as a roaring lion. Again he comes as the Accuser and whispers insinuations which harassed believers imagine proceed from themselves. Christian in *Pilgrim's Progress* was grievously beset in the Valley by such a spirit. Satan can produce a false conviction and we may mistake his voice for that of God's Spirit. In such a dark and dismal state many harassed souls fancy they have lost their salvation or have committed the unpardonable sin.

We are commanded to test such voices by the Word of God. We need not walk in such company. Submitting first to God, we must resist the devil, bidding him in the name of Christ to depart.

Do not take up with the wrong spirit. Satan apes God, and we must not be ignorant of his devices. While on your guard against the Roaring Lion, do not be deceived by the Mock Angel!

## FOLLOWERS AND FISHERS

*Follow me, and I will make you fishers of men.*
MATTHEW 4:19.

HERE IS A double-barreled combination, a command and a promise. A soul-winner is a creation of Christ, "I will make you fishers of men." Soul-winning is a product of discipleship. Jesus takes the disciple and makes not a depository but a dispenser out of him and through him reaches others. Andrew went after Peter. Philip won Nathanael. Peter fished for Cornelius, and the evangelist Philip drew in the eunuch.

Fishing for souls proceeds from following the Saviour. It is not a pursuit all by itself, to be studied and practiced independently of all else. It is a consequence of obedience, and the Lord who never fails has given His Word guaranteeing the product.

We cannot do it alone. Remember the failure of the disciples in their fishing. "Master, we have toiled all the night and have taken nothing." But when they fished at His bidding, the miracle happened. And Jesus said, "Fear not; from henceforth thou shalt catch men." It happened when Peter said, "*At thy word,* I will." "Follow *me,* and I will make you fishers of men."

## FEBRUARY 16

### ADAM AND ATOM

*Fear not them which kill the body, but are not able to kill the soul; but rather fear him which is able to destroy both soul and body in hell.* MATTHEW 10:28.

A NERVOUS GENERATION reading "What To Do If The Atom Bomb Falls" needs to be reading what to do if Judgment falls. The biggest issue is still spiritual, not atomic but Adamic, not the atom in the universe but the Adam in you and what to do about it.

Jittery humans looking for a place to hide from their own inventions had better ponder the state of their hearts before the safety of their hides. "No Hiding Place" is a common phrase now, but God is still a refuge and a shelter in time of storm.

> Rock of Ages, cleft for me,
> Let me hide myself in Thee.

Quit worrying about the atom and do something about Adam. There is a "last Adam" who can make you a new creature and give you power to become a son of God. These are beyond the reach of atoms, their true life is hid with Christ in God.


## FEBRUARY 17

### "THE END OF THE LORD"

*Ye have heard of the patience of Job, and have seen the end of the Lord.* JAMES 5:11.

THE LORD TURNED the captivity of Job and blessed the latter end of his life more than the beginning, but all that is not the climax of the book. It is not an anticlimax but it is a sort of postscript. Job arrived at the peak when he saw God. After that, whether he got well or not, or whether or not he recovered his prosperity, was incidental. He had got through to God. The main purpose of God was not to explain Job's suffering or suffering in general. Job got through to illumination, which is better than explanation.

God does not always restore our lost prosperity. Some of the greatest saints die in their poverty, their adversity and their boils. But if they have got through to God Himself, they have reached life's greatest goal. What happens after that is incidental. They are ready to say:

"Now Thee alone I seek;
Give what is best."

Do not pine away in your adversity, seeking explanation or restoration of your former prosperity. Seek to know God and thenceforth enjoy Him forever, whatever happens to your belongings and your boils!

## FEBRUARY 18

### "SPOKEN AGAINST"

*This child is set . . . for a sign which shall be spoken against.* LUKE 2:34.
*As concerning this sect, we know that everywhere it is spoken against.* ACTS 28:22.
*Blessed are ye when men shall . . . say all manner of evil against you falsely, for my sake.* MATTHEW 5:11.

THE SAVIOUR WAS spoken against. The *Sect* of His followers was spoken against. The *Saints* of any age are spoken against. We share His shame and reproach. They hated Him and they will hate us. The world hath hated us because we are not of the world. But if we be reproached as Christians, let us be happy and not ashamed (I Pt. 4:13–16).

The Beatitude of the Spoken Against has two qualifications. We are blessed not merely because we are spoken against. The charges must be false—sometimes what "they say" is true!—and it must be for Christ's sake.

The trend today is to try to make the Saviour, the Sect, and the Saints popular. But such is not the Scriptural reputation they bear. When the persecuted become the popular they are powerless. The church prospers in persecution, but pines in prosperity.

40

## GOT ANY MOUNTAINS?

*Whosoever shall say unto this mountain, Be thou re-moved and be thou cast into the sea; and shall not doubt in his heart, but shall believe that those things which he saith shall come to pass; he shall have what-soever he saith.* MARK 11:23.

CAN WE CONFIDENTLY claim and expect the conversion of our loved ones? Well, it must be in God's will. "And this is the confidence that we have in him, that, if we ask anything according to his will, he heareth us" (Jno. 5:14). Does He will the conversion of every one? "The Lord is not willing that any should perish, but that all should come to repent-ance" (II Pt. 3:9).

Then He will remove this mountain, but we must expect the mountain to move. "All things whatsoever ye shall ask in prayer, *believing*, ye shall receive" (Mt. 21:22). And the verse following our text says, "What things soever ye desire, when ye pray, *believe that ye receive them*, and ye shall have them."

We pray *hoping*, but hoping is not faith. Faith takes God's word for the deed and in its geography lists the mountain as "disappeared."

Got any mountains you think are unsinkable?

## DEPOSITORY OR DISPENSER?

*Freely ye have received, freely give.* MATTHEW 10:8.

JESUS SPEAKS OF the instructed scribe as a householder who brings forth out of his treasure things new and old. We are stewards of the manifold grace of God, not to keep it but to share it. We have a treasure in earthen vessels. The Gospel is not a secret to be hoarded but a story to be heralded. From the carcass of the lion Samson carried handfuls of honey.

Our Lord said that the Living Water should be in us a well of water springing up into everlasting life, and that from within us should flow rivers of living water. Peter said to the lame man, "Such as I have give I thee."

"To have is to owe, not own," and we are dispensers of God's grace, not depositories. It is a day of good tidings, and if we hold our peace it will go ill with us. Too many Christians are stuffing themselves with Gospel blessings, while millions have never had a taste. We are debtors to all men to give freely what we have freely received.

## FEBRUARY 21

### NO PLACE TO HIDE?

*Thou art my hiding place.* PSALM 32:7.
*Your life is hid with Christ in God.* COLOSSIANS 3:3.

A LITTLE GIRL, distressed over world conditions, wrote to a magazine editor for advice. He replied, "Let the reader grit her wisdom teeth. There is no hiding place."

It is a sad commentary on our vaunted civilization that, for all our education, science, invention, and boasted progress, we are looking for a hole in the ground in which to hide from our own devices. The theme of books and articles by, of all people, scientists is, "No Place To Hide."

But there is a hiding place. Not in a "refuge of lies" (Isa. 28:15, 17) such as we devise rather than face God. "Can any hide himself in secret places that I shall not see him?" (Jer. 23:24). Not in rocks and mountains (Rev. 6:15–17).

God is our refuge. The only way to hide from His Presence is *in* His Presence.

In the secret of His Presence
How my soul delights to hide.

He is the Haven of Rest, the Shelter in Time of Storm.

Jesus, Lover of my soul,
Let me to Thy bosom fly.

Rock of Ages, cleft for me,
Let me hide myself in Thee.

We need a refuge from the pride of man and the strife of tongues, and we may find both in the secret of His Presence (Ps. 31:20). There is a Hiding Place!

## FEBRUARY 22

### "MY HOME IS GOD"

*Lord, thou hast been our dwelling place in all generations.* PSALM 90:1.

GOD IS NOT only our hiding place, He is our dwelling place. He is not merely a Shelter for the night, He is our Staying Place forever. There we are not in hiding, we are at home.

Some flee to Him for refuge but do not make themselves at home. They worry and doubt and fear. The Israelite who worried although the blood was on his doorpost was just as safe as the one who rested in peace, but he was not enjoying his security. Blessed is the soul who learns how to nestle down deep and snug in his Abiding Place.

An old Negro woman was asked, "Are you standing on the rock, sister?" She said, "Man, I'm standing on it so solid I'm mired up in it!"

We might as well settle down in God now, for the day

will come when only God will remain. Our bodies, our homes, our financial security, our jobs, all these house us but temporarily, and one day all of them will fail. We had better be "home in God" now. Then if we lose all else we still have all we ever really had.

Your Hiding Place is your Dwelling Place. Make yourself at home!

## BELIEVE YOUR BELIEFS

*What things soever ye desire, when ye pray, believe that ye shall receive them, and ye shall have them.*
MARK 11:24.

BELIEVE THAT YOU have and you shall have—that is the grammar of faith! We are to ask for wisdom but we must ask in faith, nothing wavering (James 1:6). The believer already has all things in Christ, and by faith he lays hold of what is already his.

We must not only believe that we receive, we must believe that we believe. We must believe our beliefs and doubt our doubts. Alas, we doubt our beliefs and believe our doubts! To be always examining our faith is to destroy it. There is a strange twist of mind that afflicts some harassed souls who can never be sure of anything. These are ever learning but never able to come to a knowledge of the truth.

We must give ourselves credit for such faith as we can muster. The father of the demonized boy said to our Lord, "Lord, I believe; help thou mine unbelief." His faith was weak and mixed with unbelief and he knew it, but he knew that he had at least a little faith and that faith he asserted. Of course, our faith, like every other good and perfect gift,

44

is of God, but God expects us to use it, affirm it, not doubt it. "If thou canst believe" implies that we can if we will. God would not ask us to believe if we could not.

## GOD'S GEOGRAPHY

*He brought me forth also into a large place.*
PSALM 18:19.

IT MAY BE only a pin-point on the map but if it is the Lord's place for us, it is a large place. God's geography does not read like ours. His ways are not our ways and His standards of greatness and success are foolish to this world. An obscure country church, even the bedroom of an invalid, may be a great place if it is the place of His will and lit with His presence.

And anywhere we may go, it is a large place if God be with us.

> To me remains nor place nor time;
> My country is in every clime;
> I can be calm and free from care
> On any shore, since God is there.

Madame Guyon found that God makes the place. Watch your harassed tourist trying to get away from it all. Alas, it matters not where he goes, he has to take himself along and there lies the problem. But

> All scenes alike engaging prove
> To souls impressed with sacred love.

45

Blessed is he who travels by God's geography. With him a stone pillow in a strange land may mark the house of God and the gate to heaven.

## THE BEATITUDE OF THE "AND YETS"

*Thomas, because thou hast seen me, thou hast believed; blessed are they that have not seen, and yet have believed.* JOHN 20:29.

THOMAS COULD HAVE made a great story of his experience, for few ever had such a privilege as he. But our Lord did not magnify it: rather He magnified the commoner experience of believing without seeing. All of us can claim that beatitude! It is not so glamorous and it does not make a sensational story, but precious in the sight of the Lord are His saints who can relate no amazing experiences but who believe, anyway.

Peter sensed the importance of walking by faith instead of sight when he wrote, "Whom having not seen ye love; in whom, though now ye see him not, *yet believing*, ye rejoice with joy unspeakable and full of glory."

*And yet have believed . . . yet believing.* There was only one Thomas who could put his finger in the nailprints of the Saviour but their number is legion who have believed without seeing. For reasons best known to Himself our Lord sometimes gives extra tokens to one now and then, but it is very evident that He values highly those who get along without them. Ours is the beatitude of the *and yets,* and in its blessing we carry on until we see Him as He is.

46

## FEBRUARY 26

### "NOWHERE" OR "NOW HERE'"

*The fool hath said in his heart, There is no God.*
PSALM 14:1.
*Emmanuel . . . God with us.* MATTHEW 1:23.
*He dwelleth with you, and shall be in you.* JOHN 14:17.

AN ATHEIST HAD a sign on the wall of his office that read, "God Is Nowhere." A little girl saw it and exclaimed, "Look! It says, 'God Is Now Here!' "

Today godless and lawless millions deny God's very existence. But there are still many who have not bowed to this Baal, who know that the Word became flesh and that in the Holy Spirit God is not only with us but in us.

The struggle is between the "Nowheres" and the "Now Heres." "Is the Lord among us, or not?" (Ex. 17:7)—that is the issue. The fool hath said in his heart, "There is no God," because God is not in his heart. The Christian says there is a God, because God is in his heart. He means more than merely that God is or that God is somewhere. He says God is now here, because God is a present, living reality.

> You ask me how I know He lives,
> He lives within my heart!

These are they who know that the tabernacle of the Lord is with men because He lives in us, the temples of His Holy Spirit.

### FEBRUARY 27

### "THEN JESUS CAME"

*When the doors were shut . . . came Jesus . . .*
*Came Jesus, the doors being shut.* JOHN 20:19, 26.

ARE YOU LIVING behind closed doors bolted against some nameless dread or fear? Is it fear of man, fear of tomorrow,

47

or some other hobgoblin that peers in the window of your soul? The Lord is with you. Not visibly as in this blessed account, but remember that He told Thomas on this same day. "Blessed are they that have not seen, and yet have believed." You can count on Him, for He promised to be with us all the days—all kinds of days.

No prison bars, no dungeon gates, no walls of blindness, deafness, no Patmos isles of loneliness can keep Him out. The doors being shut . . . comes Jesus! "He saw them toiling in rowing . . . and . . . he cometh unto them." Our very distress is the reason for His approach! The very fact that the doors are shut challenges Him to enter!

There is only one door He will not enter—your unyielded heart. But open that door and He will come in. All other closed doors are to Him an invitation, not a barrier.

"Came Jesus . . . the doors being shut."

## FEBRUARY 28

### HAPPINESS OR HAPPEN-NESS?

*The things which happened unto me have fallen out rather unto the furtherance of the Gospel.* Philippians 1:12.
*Rejoice in the Lord always and again I say, Rejoice.* Philippians 4:4.

"Which happened" is not in the original, but the idea is. This world's happiness should be spelled "happenness," because it depends on what happens. Paul's joy was not over the things which had happened unto him, things the world would call calamities. Yet he was happy because he knew that all things work together for good to the Christian. What men mean for evil God turns to good, as He did with Joseph.

So amidst all these adverse "happenings" Paul can write from prison, "Rejoice in the Lord alway: and again I say,

48

Rejoice." What this world calls happiness is not what God calls joy. His joy is the bequest of a Man of sorrows acquainted with grief, made available to us by His death on a cross. It is a deep, strange joy that may fill the heart when eyes are filled with tears. It is a heavenly joy beyond the tyranny of what happens and the whims of circumstance. It abides even when our feelings call us liars.

Thank God for "happiness—whatever happens."

## FEBRUARY 29

### ORPAH OR RUTH?

*And Orpah kissed her mother-in-law; but Ruth clave unto her.* RUTH 1:14.

WE PROVE OUR love by our loyalty. Orpah made a show of affection, but it was Ruth who said, "Whither thou goest I will go; and where thou lodgest, I will lodge: thy people shall be my people and thy God my God."

Judas betrayed the Lord with a kiss, not a slap. Our Lord is betrayed with a show of affection perhaps more often than in any other way. We call Him Lord, Lord, and do not what He says. He that keepeth His commandments, he it is that loveth Him, not he that just sings "O, How I Love Jesus."

As with the woman who cried out in the crowd (Lk. 11: 27, 28) and Mary in the garden (Jno. 20:17), our Lord attaches little importance to an outward show of affection, but makes obedience to His commands the primary matter. To be sure, He welcomes our kiss: "Thou gavest me no kiss; but this woman . . . hath not ceased to kiss my feet" (Lk. 7:45); but as with husband and wife so it is with the soul and Christ, the test of love is loyalty.

There are Sunday-morning Orpahs aplenty, but few Ruths who cleave unto Jesus wherever He goes, who make His people their people and His God their God.

49

## RESIGNATION OR ACCEPTANCE?

*It is the Lord: let him do what seemeth him good.*
I SAMUEL 3:18.

ELI WAS RESIGNED to the will of God as revealed by Samuel. Resignation is better than rebellion or a stiff-upper-lip Stoicism, but it is not the highest attitude. We acquiesce and resign to the inevitable because we have to! After all, there isn't much we can do about it.

Resignation may bring a martyr complex and a selfish pride at putting up with whatever comes. Better than all this is acceptance: accept the will of God when adversity comes, learn whatever lessons are in it and believe that it works for our good. That is a wholesome and healthy spirit. Rebellion or a mere endurance of affliction may wreck us. Resignation may make us "proud that we are humble." Acceptance falls in with God's plan and purpose and enables us to safely trust, even though we may not fully understand.

Some things, of course, are never meant to be accepted. They are the will of the devil and must be resisted and defeated. But that which cannot be changed may be turned to God's glory and our good if accepted and transmuted from a burden into a blessing.

## MARCH 2

## CLAIMING OUR RIGHTS

*I appeal unto Cæsar.* ACTS 25:11.

WE ARE TO render unto Cæsar the things which are Cæsar's, and there are times when we may appeal unto Cæsar. Not claiming our own rights does not mean that we should not avail ourselves of certain privileges as citizens and otherwise. Paul did not court martyrdom, and he defended himself ably on trial. He used all his standing as a Roman citizen and employed every means to get fair treatment. When persecuted in one city we are to flee to another. We may honor God more by living than by dying. A supine acceptance of circumstances that could be, and ought to be, changed is not a mark of piety. We are not always to remain quiet and expect God to intervene when He has given us common sense to ask for normal rights to which we are entitled. Christians are not to go to law with each other, and for the sake of our testimony it is better at times to suffer ourselves to be defrauded. But the cause of the Gospel is often advanced, as it was with Paul in our text, by asserting our claim to certain rights. Some may have thought it nobler if Paul had let things take their course, without speaking up for himself. God did not think so, for He wanted Paul to go to Rome.

There is a time to appeal unto Cæsar.


## MARCH 3

### PATTERN FOR REVIVAL

*Restore unto me the joy of thy salvation; and uphold me with thy free spirit. Then will I teach transgressors thy ways; and sinners shall be converted unto thee.*
PSALM 51:12, 13.

HERE IN OLD TESTAMENT language is the difference between revival and evangelism, so often confused today. David is saying, "Make me right and then I will go after somebody else!" Too much church work is being done by people who

51

are not right with God and each other, who know neither the joy of salvation nor a willing spirit.

Conviction of sin, confession of sin, cleansing, and a right spirit—all this is revival. Evangelism, soul-winning, personal work, the conversion of sinners—all this flows from revival.

David needed a Nathan, and the church needs a prophet to tell his story and make the application, "Thou art the man." That is not easy—especially if "the man" is sitting right in front of you! There are guilty Davids aplenty but few faithful Nathans.

## MARCH 4

### "THEY NEED NOT DEPART"

*They need not depart; give ye them to eat.* MATTHEW 14:16.

THE DISCIPLES THOUGHT it was time to send the multitude away to buy food. But it is never necessary to go away from Jesus for anything. All we need is in Him. Men are going in all directions foraging for food, but He is the Bread of Life. It is not necessary to supplement your diet with anything from the fleshpots of Egypt. All the vitamins and calories your soul requires are in Christ. He is Alpha and Omega—and all the letters between!

But He also said, "Give ye them to eat." We are His agents, His representatives today, and we need never send men away elsewhere from our sufficient Saviour.

But how can we give them to eat? The disciples saw only five loaves and two fishes. The Lord said, "Bring them hither to me." Bring what you have, all you have, and He will multiply it to meet the demand.

What a joy to represent a Lord who never meets an emergency that makes it necessary to dismiss the crowd! They need never depart—for to whom shall they go?

## MARCH 5

### "YOU KNOW HOW IT IS"

*He knoweth our frame; he remembereth that we are dust.* PSALM 103:14.

HAVE YOU COME to the end of a very imperfect day, when everything has gone wrong, unable at night to put together a sensible prayer? Finally, you gave up trying and lumped the whole tangled mess and committed it to an understanding God, while you sighed very lamely, "Lord, you know how it is."

He does. And what a blessed relief to know that when we do the best we can, not faultlessly but blamelessly, He takes all the loose ends and ragged edges and binds them into a perfect whole. For we are complete in Him.

And I smiled to think God's greatness
Flows around our incompleteness;
'Round our restlessness His rest.

He makes up all the deficiencies, and rounds out all the broken corners. He knows the heart's intent and credits the soul's sincere desire, though it be poorly expressed in the deed. As Whittier put it, He judges our frailty by the life we meant.

This affords no ground for slovenliness. Do your very best. But remember that your very best is very poor. He will perfect it in Himself.

He knows how it is.

53

## MARCH 6

### NOT NOW BUT AFTERWARDS

*What I do thou knowest not now; but thou shalt know
hereafter.* JOHN 13:7.

OUR LORD'S SAYING goes deeper than the immediate application of this precious word. God trusts some of His
saints in the dark. To some He allows chapters that defy
all explanation, that do not make sense, that seem to con-
tradict all we have been taught to expect. From some He
seems to withdraw His presence; some He lets pass from
this world in strange and sinister ways. We must never
make too much of deathbed stories, for some choice saints
have had anything but a shouting exit.

We must take account of this, for all lives do not follow
the course we would have anticipated. Paul dropped from
height to depth in the same chapter (II Cor. 12), from
third heaven to thorn in the flesh, and God may give us
along with a mountain-top vision a dark valley where deliverance is not granted.

Some chapters are to be experienced now and understood hereafter. It is well to be forewarned about them
and forearmed for them, even if they do not come, lest
Satan overwhelm us as he sought to do with Job and Peter.
God marks across some of our days, "Will explain later."

## MARCH 7

### FAIR-WEATHER REPENTANCE

*The goodness of God leadeth thee to repentance.*
ROMANS 2:4.

WE OUGHT NOT wait for the hour of trial, the time of
chastening, to set our house in order, to take stock of ourselves, to have our commission renewed. God's goodness,

not His scourging alone, is meant to lead us to repentance The day of blessing should bring us to the mourner's bench, and then we might avert the painful discipline. If we judged ourselves in the sunshine we might not be judged in the shadow.

Thatch your roof in dry weather. Do not wait until the storm breaks. While you have health and loved ones and prosperity, let the Great Physician give you a check-up. Do not wait until you are grievously smitten.

Though most of us come to conversion and confession and cleansing in the hour of desperation, it need not be so. God's goodness ought to melt our hearts and break us down and shame our lack of faith and our love grown cold.

Fair-weather repentance might save us many a cloudy day.

## MARCH 8

### WHAT TO DO WITH YOURSELF

*We had the sentence of death in ourselves, that we should not trust in ourselves, but in God which raiseth the dead.* II CORINTHIANS 1:9.

"COMING TO THE end of self," a phrase much used in some circles, is not a Bible phrase, but what is meant by it is Biblical. The Scriptures speak of denying self (Mt. 16:24), judging one's self (I Cor. 11:31), the crucifixion of self (Rom. 6:6; Gal. 5:24).

So few Christians ever get out of themselves into Him. They live a changed life but not the exchanged life—"not I but Christ." We must come to the end of our experiences, our success, our prayers, our seeking and striving, all that we can see or feel, to where our comeliness is turned to corruption and we can only cry, "Woe is *me!*" There is no lib

55

erty and victory until we cease from our own works and settle down in God.

In this day of self-exaltation the Bible teaches self-execution. Not that we execute ourselves but that we submit to the death of self by the hand of God. Paul witnessed his own execution, but there came forth a new Paul, "I live, yet not I, but Christ liveth in me".

What to do with yourself? Agree and submit to your execution!

## MARCH 9

### BE YOUR AGE

*That we henceforth be no more children.* EPHESIANS 4:14.

WE ARE TO be childlike (Mt. 18:3) but not childish (Mt. 11:16). Those who pursue the study of the deeper Christian life often miss the way and become Faddists, studying it as a novelty, playing with it, like the world plays bridge. Others become Freaks, going off at tangents on "death to self" or the filling of the Spirit or some other point, making the part greater than the whole. Still others become Failures, giving up the whole thing in disillusionment.

There are not enough wholesome, healthy, normal Christians who "grow up." We either freeze or fry, it seems. What a picture Paul paints here of saints and churches, carried about with every wind of doctrine instead of maturing in Christ! And we grow up in *Him*, Christ in His fulness, not in some phase or feature of His fulness, however precious. How many saints, babes on milk instead of meat, need to "be their age!"

56

## MARCH 10

### "VIVAL" OR REVIVAL?

*Enoch walked with God.* GENESIS 5:24.

ENOCH DID NOT need a revival every year to keep him going. Most Christians and churches need a periodic stirring up, but it should not, and need not, be so. We are in danger of thinking of revival as an occasional shot in the arm, a spurt of religious enthusiasm that soon plays out. God never meant that His children should live by fits and starts, an up-and-down experience. Some husbands and wives live that way, with periods of indifference, quarreling, and then making up again. How much better is that steady and constant companionship, not perfect, but faithful and dependable day by day!

With churches on almost every other corner, it is pathetic that we should have to have a special reviving every year. If we walked with God and kept up to date with Him we should never need to call in a preacher to get us back to normal. For real revival is simply normal New Testament Christianity, not an unusual religious spree.

If we had a daily "vival" we should not need an occasional revival. Let us walk as children of the day and we shall not need to be awakened every year.

## MARCH 11

### "WITHOUT ME—NOTHING"

*Without me ye can do nothing.* JOHN 15:5.

THE STARTING POINT to "all things" is to learn that we are nothing. "For I know that in me (that is, in my flesh) dwelleth no good thing" (Rom. 7:18). "For if a man think himself to be something, when he is nothing, he deceiveth himself" (Gal. 6:3). What a self-deceived generation, then, is ours!

"It is not in man that walketh to direct his steps." We do not have what it takes. Start with your nothingness—"Just as I am, without one plea"—and you are on your way to His "all things."

> Let our debts be what they may, however great or small;
> As soon as we have naught to pay, our Lord forgives us all.
> 'Tis perfect poverty alone that sets the soul at large;
> While we can call one mite our own, we have no full discharge.

We can never be blessed until we learn that we can bring nothing to Christ but our need. "All the fitness He requireth is to feel your need of Him."

## MARCH 12

### "WITH HIM—ALL THINGS"

*He that spared not his own Son, but delivered him up for us all, how shall he not with him freely give us all things?* ROMANS 8:32.

How BLESSED TO move from our nothingness to "everything in Jesus"! "By him all things consist." The Father has given him all things ( Jno. 3:35; 13:3; 16:15). All things were made by him ( Jno. 1:3; I Cor. 8:6). Jesus has said, "All things are mine . . . Come" (Mt. 11:27, 28); "All things are mine . . . Believe" (Jno. 3:35, 36); "All things are mine . . . Go" (Mt. 28:18–20).

Your part is to bring Him all your need. His part is to supply all your need (Phil. 4:19). If the first step is to realize the nothingness of yourself, the second is to turn to the Allness of Christ.

"All that I need is Jesus," because all that I need is in Jesus. If God spared not His own Son but freely delivered Him up for our redemption, He will not give me the greater and fail to give me the lesser, but with Him He has given all else that I need, whether great or small.

And if everything is in Jesus, surely Jesus ought to be everything to us!

## MARCH 13

### "ALL THINGS ARE YOURS"

*For all things are yours; whether Paul, or Apollos, or Cephas, or the world, or life, or death, or things present, or things to come; all are yours. And ye are Christ's; and Christ is God's.* I CORINTHIANS 3:21–23.

THEN TAKE HIM for everything, salvation, strength, guidance, every need of the whole man. "Having nothing, and yet possessing all things" (II Cor. 6:10)—blessed paradox! I bring Him my nothingness and take His Allness. "Nothing in my hand I bring, simply to Thy cross I cling." From nothing to everything!

And there is power to do. "I can do all things through Christ which strengtheneth me" (Phil. 4:13). For God is able to make all grace abound toward me, that I always having all sufficiency in all things, may abound to every good work (II Cor. 9:8).

I am not just to enjoy all this for myself. All things are mine except myself. I am not my own, I am bought with a price; therefore I ought to glorify God in my body and in my spirit, which are God's (I Cor. 6:19, 20).

Move out of Nothing into Everything! It is all in Christ and it is all for you. And you are then not a depository but a dispenser. "Freely ye have received, freely give."

59

## MARCH 14

### A TRYST WITH GOD

*And the Lord spake unto Moses face to face, as a man speaketh unto his friend.* EXODUS 33:11.

THE MEN GOD has used most through the ages bear one common mark—at some time in their lives they came to a tryst with God, to a secret understanding with the Most High. They had a private meeting with the Eternal, a rendezvous with the Almighty. The Bible carries a series of such experiences, from Genesis to Revelation. The pages of church history abound with such records.

Such men come to God alone, like Jacob at Jabbok, Moses in Midian, John on Patmos. Eagles do not fly in droves. After waiting on God, these men mounted on wings as eagles.

"After *he* had seen the vision, immediately *we* endeavored to go" (Acts 16:10). The vision does not come to the crowd but to the individual. Moses met God, and then the people followed Moses. No man is prepared to meet the people until first he has met God. Our Lord Himself began a busy day in the desert alone at prayer.

Begin your life work, begin your day, with God.


### MARCH 15

### ARE YOU THIRSTY?

*O God, thou art my God; early will I seek thee; my soul thirsteth for thee, my flesh longeth for thee in a dry and thirsty land, where no water is.* PSALM 63:1.

A DRY LAND, a thirsty soul, and a satisfying God (v. 5, "My soul shall be satisfied"). "He satisfieth the longing soul and filleth the hungry soul with goodness" (Ps. 107:9). How barren is the land with its broken cisterns that can hold no water!

Does your soul pant after God as the hart pants after the water brooks? "Blessed are they that hunger and thirst after righteousness, for they shall be filled." They are blessed because they shall be filled! "If any man thirst, let him come unto me, and drink" (Jno. 7:37).

A Satisfying God. "O God, thou art *my* God." A lot of praying gets no further than "O God." There is the personal appropriation, "Thou art *my* God!"

"Early will I seek thee." "Those that seek me early shall find me" (Prov. 8:17). Early in life: "Remember thy Creator in the days of thy youth." Early in the day like Jesus in the morning.

## MARCH 16

### SHOWCASE AND SHELVES

*A friend of mine in his journey is come to me, and I have nothing to set before him.* LUKE 11:6.

MANY A CHRISTIAN, many a church, has everything in the showcase and nothing on the shelves. The customers come in, but everything is in the window. We have nothing in stock, no spiritual reserves, no Divine supplies, no bread from heaven.

"Therefore every scribe which is instructed unto the kingdom of heaven is like a man that is an householder, which bringeth forth out of his treasure things new and old" (Mt. 13:52). Change it to "storekeeper" and the lesson is the same. But what if we have no treasure, no goods on hand?

True, we are dispensers, not depositories, and we are to relay the bread from God to men, fresh bread, not stale. But there must be a deposit if we are to dispense. We should have a stock of Scripture, of experience, of grace, treasure in earthen vessels that we may have to give to him that needeth.

Pity the church with everything in the show window and showcase, where the hungry come and find but a shell, nothing in stock!

## MARCH 17

### THE UNSCHEDULED MIRACLE

*Now Peter and John went up together into the temple at the hour of prayer. . . . And a certain man lame from his mother's womb was carried, whom they laid daily at the gate of the temple.* Acts 3:1, 2.

THE HEALING OF the lame man was not on anybody's schedule that morning. Peter and John never dreamed, when they set out, what a tempestuous day it would be. The lame man did not know it was to be his red-letter day. The people of Jerusalem never imagined the city would be in an upheaval before sundown. Peter and John had gone up to pray, but the unscheduled event became the main event.

When we are in the path of duty we are on the high-road of blessing. Anything may happen. And the blessing by the way may eclipse what we set out to obtain. The healing of the lame man was a side line that morning but soon took the main line.

When you walk in His will the unscheduled thing you did not know about when you set out may bring greater blessing than the main objective you had in mind. Our Father is the God of the Unexpected and His schedule has items not listed on ours.

## WHEN THE SUPPLY SEEMS INADEQUATE

*They say unto him, We have here but five loaves and two fishes. He said, Bring them hither to me.* MATTHEW 14:17, 18.

JESUS HAD TOLD His disciples to feed the hungry multitude. But their resources seemed utterly inadequate to the demand—and the command.

Has the Lord commissioned you to a task for which you have not the wherewithal? As with the man in the parable, have your friends come to you in their journey and you have nothing to set before them? Are you wondering how in the world to stretch your loaves and fishes to feed so many hungry mouths? Your family, your life work, your church, your Bible class—you look at your pitiful resources and sigh, "What are they among so many?"

"Bring them hither to me." Little is much when He takes over. "Who is sufficient for these things? Our sufficiency is of God." But all our efficiency without His sufficiency is only a deficiency.

There were basketfuls left over. God always gives overflowing measure, "good measure, pressed down, and shaken together and running over." He giveth liberally, exceedingly abundantly, above all that we can ask or think. He will turn your scarcity into a surplus. Bring it to Him.

## WHEN THE CASE SEEMS IMPOSSIBLE

*I brought him to thy disciples, and they could not cure him. Then Jesus answered, and said . . . Bring him hither to me.* MATTHEW 17:16, 17.

"AND THEY COULD not"—it is helpless disciples against a demon, a powerless church before a devil-possessed world, our plight before many a situation. But however much Christians and churches may fail, Christ does not fail—"Bring him hither to me." What if the father, disappointed at the disciples' failure, had taken the boy away?

When you face a case that seems hopeless bring it to Jesus. His touch has still its ancient power. And His power is available to us. When the disciples asked, "Why could not we cast him out?" Jesus answered, "Because of your unbelief: for verily I say unto you, If ye have faith as a grain of mustard seed, ye shall say unto this mountain, Remove hence to yonder place; and it shall remove; and nothing shall be impossible unto you. Howbeit this kind goeth not out but by prayer and fasting."

Faith and prayer will move the mountain and drive out the demon. "With God all things are possible." "All things are possible to him that believeth."

## MARCH 20

### WHEN THE TASK SEEMS INSIGNIFICANT

*Go ye into the village over against you: in the which at your entering ye shall find a colt tied, whereon yet never man sat: loose him, and bring him hither.* LUKE 19:30.

THESE DISCIPLES, AFTER three years of training for greater tasks, might have felt that going after a donkey was a rather unimportant errand. But there are no trivial assignments in the work of the Lord. That colt was part of the Divine plan from the foundation of the world. The Lord of creation called it into His service just as He called to His service the fish with the tax money in its mouth and the rooster at Peter's denial.

64

If you are commissioned to go "borrow a colt" for the Lord do not think your chore has no significance. Bring the colt to Him and He will fit it into His arrangements. The simplest detail is charged with meaning if it be part of His will. This humble little colt was a fulfilment of prophecy made centuries before, and the smallest link in the chain of God's great purpose is worth your service.

They were to tell the owner of the colt, "The Lord hath need of him." Finding a few loaves and fishes for Him to bless and multiply, a fish with a coin to pay His taxes, a donkey for Him to ride—nothing is too lowly if the Lord needs it.

## MARCH 21

### THE FAIR KING AND THE FAR COUNTRY

*Thine eyes shall see the king in his beauty: they shall behold the land that is very far off.* ISAIAH 33:17.

THE VISION OF the King is followed by the View of The Land of Far Distances. After the Vision, the Vista. First, there is the Christian life itself opening up in all its limit-'ess outreaches. We need not stand on Jordan's stormy banks casting a wishful eye to Canaan's fair and happy land, where our possessions lie. Canaan for the Christian is not heaven beyond but the heavenlies now, and he may follow his Joshua ("Jesus" is the same name) across Jordan and possess his possessions. The life that is hid with Christ in God is boundless in its possibilities, even in its earthly chapter now before the believer gets to glory.

Alas, too many of us are slack to possess the Promised Land. Like the Israelites in Canaan, we settle down in a little portion of it and compromise with what we should conquer. The average Christian needs to see the Far

Country of a life of spiritual victory wherein we reign now as well as after death. Blessed is he who having seen the King sees also what he himself may be now, as well as what he may become hereafter!

It is well to read in Revelation of what lies in the millennium ahead. It is also glorious to see in Ephesians the far country visible from the milestones today.

## MARCH 22

### ANOTHER FAR COUNTRY

*Go ye into all the world.* MARK 16:15.

WE ARE NOT only to see the King, we must serve the King. And the far country of service is as big as the world, for the world is our parish. Your own part of the Lord's vineyard may be across the sea or just across the street, but what you do may reach around the earth.

Every Christian is a missionary, for all the world is a mission field. Do not think of missionaries as meaning only those witnesses abroad who have returned from Africa or Asia with pictures to show to sleepy church members in an after-meeting. If you cannot cross the sea in person you can project yourself by prayer and provision. You can pray laborers into the harvest and you can provide for them while they are in the harvest. The smallest country church may have a world-wide ministry and the lowliest Christian may touch earth's uttermost corner.

"After he had seen the vision, immediately we endeavored to go" (Acts 16:10). The Vision, the Vista, the Venture. The "Lo" must be followed by the "Go." Isaiah saw the King. He saw the country, "a people of unclean lips." He heard the call, "Whom shall I send?" He answered it: "Here am I, send me."

66

The Far Country of the Heavenlies has its counterpart in the Far Country of the Earthlies. The Mystery must be made known amidst the Misery!

## MARCH 23

### THE GREATEST FAR COUNTRY

*I saw a new heaven and a new earth.*
REVELATION 21:1.

HERE IS THE fairest vista of all after the vision of the Fair King—the life beyond, all eternity "with the Lord." It is the person who makes the place. Paradise, heaven, the new earth, there is much we do not understand about these, but we know that He said, "Today shalt thou be *with me.*" "*Where* I *am,* there ye may be also."

For the new creature in Christ "old things are passed away"—the old things of sin. John saw a new heaven and earth, "for the first heaven and the first earth were passed away"—the old creation has gone. He also observed that "there shall be no more death, neither sorrow, nor crying, neither shall there be any more pain: for the former things are passed away." The Christian outlasts all that went with the old Adam, for he belongs to the new creation of the last Adam. "The world passeth away and the lust thereof: but he that doeth the will of God abideth forever."

Just as we first see, then serve, the King in the Far Country of the Christian life and the Far Country of Christian witnessing, so in the greatest Far Country of all, the world beyond, "his servants shall serve him." Not a glorified vacation but a glorious vocation; no longer hindered by the limitations of the old Adam, we shall see Him as He is and serve Him as we should.

## MARCH 24

### WITH OR AGAINST?

*He that is not with me is against me; and he that gath-
ereth not with me scattereth abroad.* MATTHEW 12:30.

IT IS NOT correct to ask, 'What will you do with Jesus?"
Rather, the issue is, "What are you doing about Him now?"
There is no neutral ground. We are with Him or against
Him. And we gather or scatter.

There are no "inactive" church members. A Negro pastor
whose flock numbered one hundred was asked how many
active members he had. "One hundred," he replied; "Fifty
active for me and fifty active against me."

It is not possible to be inwardly and secretly for Christ
without being active for Him. "I never work at my religion,
but I am not against Christ." Yes, you are. If you are not
gathering you are scattering. If you are not working in some
way with the Great Gatherer, winning souls and fishing for
men, you are an instrument of division, opposed to the only
true unifying force in the universe.

Gatherers and scatterers—it comes down to that, and
there are only two kinds of people. The first half of our
verse sets forth the real issue today—"with me, against me"
—Christ or Antichrist. And we are either Christians or Anti-
christians, not just non-Christians.

Are you with Him or against Him? If you gather not with
Him you scatter abroad.

## MARCH 25

### LIVING PERMANENCE

*He shall be like a tree planted by the rivers of water.*
PSALM 1:3.

THE RIGHTEOUS MAN is not like a tombstone but like a tree.
A tombstone is permanent, but it is dead permanence. A

tree has living permanence, it is planted, not merely put, by the rivers of water.

The Psalmist said, "My heart is fixed." Some saints have fixed heads, they are steadfast and unmovable, but it is the fixity of stubbornness and obstinacy. "Nothing is more like real conviction than simple obstinacy." So much of orthodoxy is the tombstone kind. We tend to petrify. Religious movements run a certain course—a man, a movement, a machine, a monument. Churches tend to become like trees in the Petrified Forest instead of living trees by the rivers of water.

Our faith, too, must be like seed, not sand, for living permanence endures because it perpetuates itself. A stone remains a stone. The Gospel reproduces itself from life to life. Christ lives from generation to generation, not only in heaven but in the hearts of His people.

## MARCH 26

### GOD'S FINISHED PRODUCT

*The Lord will perfect that which concerneth me.*
PSALM 138:8.

I HAVE HEARD of a little boy whose sailor father was coming home to see him. The youngster worked the afternoon long trying to carve a ship model from a block of wood. He fell asleep, with very little success achieved for all his whittling. That night his father came, removed the block of wood and put in its place a real wooden ship exquisitely carved and rigged to perfection.

Your life and mine often bears poor resemblance to the Perfect Model. At our best we are like the carving of the little boy. But one day we shall awake in His likeness and see Him as He is. And we shall find that we bear the image

69

of the heavenly. He who has begun a good work in us in regeneration will perform it in sanctification until the day of Jesus Christ in glorification. We were predestinated to be conformed to the image of God's Son, and God will make of us a finished product and a perfect creation.

It will be great to awaken in the morning and find that we are just like Jesus!

Cheer up, my brother. He will perfect that which concerneth you!

## MARCH 27

### THE SUPREME EXPERIENCE

*My grace is sufficient for thee.* II CORINTHIANS 12:9.

WITHIN A FEW verses Paul goes from height to depth and rises again to greater height than ever. His third heaven experience, his thorn in the flesh, his denied request, should settle once for all what is the supreme matter in this earthly sojourn. We like to play up third heavens, mighty deliverances, amazing answers to prayer. The supreme experience of Paul was none of these but a constant dependence on God's sufficient grace. That does not sound spectacular, sensational; it does not make as good a story as third heavens and startling deliverances, but God rates it higher. After all, in the strength of it Paul outtraveled, outpreached, outwrote, and, in general, outperformed any man of his day.

It is better to be buffeted by Satan's messenger than to be exalted above measure by a third heaven experience. Better have something you can tell than hear words you cannot utter! Life's greatest experience is to live in the strength of Another the Exchanged Life—"Christ liveth in me." It is better for heaven thus to come to earth than for you temporarily to be caught up to heaven.

70

# MARCH 28

## DRAB DAY

*Lo, I am with you alway [all the days], even unto the end of the world.* MATTHEW 28:20.

"ALL THE DAYS," any day, every day, all kinds of days, His grace is sufficient. And no days prove Him more than the dull, dry, tedious days when time hangs heavy on our hands, when nothing seems to happen, when the hands of the clock seem stuck, so slowly move the hours.

I write today in a drab small-town railroad depot where I must wait six hours for a train. Too cold to walk outside, nothing to see, nothing to do. Nothing to do? There is always an opportunity of some sort to buy up in these days so evil. There is a Bible to read, a Heavenly Father to whom we may pray. A good book to read—in this case Marcus Rainsford's *Our Lord Prays For His Own*. An old man came in and I had a word with him about the Lord. Now I'm writing this bit. There is time to meditate. A humdrum day may be no less a holy day and a happy day. He is with us all the days—including this one! And this is the day which the Lord hath made.

I am steward of my days, and it is required of a steward that he be found faithful. This is the only day of its kind. It will never come again. And as in any other day, there are hours to prove His presence and enjoy His sufficient grace.

# MARCH 29

## WHEN THE CRASH COMES

*And there was a day . . .* JOB 1:13.

AND WHAT A day that was! Job's possessions and children swept away within a few hours! It was such a day as Jacob had when his sons reported Joseph slain. Such a day as came to David with the death of his beloved Absalom.

There will come such days. Very few escape them. Castles tumble. The savings of a lifetime vanish. The doctor says there is no hope.

When the crash comes Jacob may lament, "All these things are against me." But, later, Joseph may say, "Ye thought evil . . . but God meant it unto good."

The grace of God is sufficient for the disastrous day as well as for the drab day when nothing happens. Our Lord asked that His disciples be kept by the Father (John 17:11), and they were. Yet they were not spared adversity and for most of them there was violent death. He kept them and none was lost save the son of perdition. His keeping may include days when all seems to collapse. The body, even the mind, may fail. But He takes care of the real "us," though the outward man perish.

It was an awful day for Job. But it led to his greatest day, when he saw God.


## MARCH 30

### WHEN EVERYTHING GOES WRONG

*Thou art careful and troubled about many things.*
Luke 10:41.

I do not know what had gone wrong in the kitchen, but it was "one of those days." Not a drab, uneventful day—plenty happens on these distracting days, when we seem to have got out on the wrong side of the bed. All day long we are vexed and pestered by the mosquitoes of petty care. Everything seems to have determined to be perverse. Tempers flare, nerves are strained, we "feel like we could scream."

Some people can stand big troubles better than this variety. They rise to the crash and disaster, but the wear and tear of petty distractions overcome them. And yet perhaps it is a greater victory to overcome these little aggravations than to face nobly a gigantic trial.

There is grace for these days too. We may be kept in perfect peace if our minds are stayed on Him. These dwarfish demons can do our testimony more harm than the onslaught of an oversized devil. The breakfast table may call for more grace than the Lord's table on Sunday morning. Instead of depending on two cups of coffee making you fit to live with, get a good start at the feet of the Lord of "all the days."

## MARCH 31

### DARK DAY

*Who is among you that . . . walketh in darkness and hath no light? let him trust in the name of the Lord, and stay upon his God.* ISAIAH 50:10.

THESE ARE NOT merely days of disaster but days of darkness, when there is no sense of God's presence, when He seems to hide His face. Like Job, we go forward, but He is not there; and backward, but we cannot perceive Him: on the left hand, where He doth work, but we cannot behold Him; and He hideth Himself on the right hand, that we cannot see Him.

These are the days when the unexplainable happens, the dark sinister thing that doesn't make sense, when our experience is against us, when we can feel no inspiration, when all we have believed seems crushed and Satan laughs and tells us our faith is a fraud.

God trusts some of His children with a walk in the dark. They may even so leave this world. But He will raise them all in the morning. And never do we glorify Him more than when we trust in His Name and stay upon Him, anyhow, come what may, regardless.

## APRIL 1

### GARMENTS OF GREY

*Thou shalt not wear a garment of divers sorts, as of woolen and linen together.* DEUTERONOMY 22:11.
*Let thy garments be always white.* ECCLESIASTES 9:8.

JOWETT SAYS, "Worldly compromise takes the medium line between white and black and wears an ambiguous gray." An American statesman says, "The values of life which were clear to the Pilgrims and the Founding Fathers have become dim and fuzzy in outline."

We live today in a twilight zone, a hazy condition of low visibility. Black and white have become a smudge of indefinite grey.

God despises mixtures. Our Lord says He will spew the lukewarm out of His mouth—and lukewarm is another word for the same state of compromise.

"Abhor that which is evil." The fear of the Lord is to hate evil." "He that is not with me is against me." There is no mild tolerance here.

God abominates garments of gray. If we are to wear white hereafter, better practice it here!


## APRIL 2

### "COME AND SEE"

*And Nathanael said unto him, Can there any good thing come out of Nazareth? Philip saith unto him, Come and see.* JOHN 1:46.

PHILIP DID NOT let Nathanael sidetrack him into a discussion of whether or not any good thing could come out of Nazareth. That was irrelevant and Philip was no authority on the matter. After all, the best way to settle that question,

74

as well as all others, was, "Come and see for yourself."
Jesus was just out of Nazareth, and Nathanael could soon
find out the answer to his query.

The devil likes to sidetrack us from the real issue. The
woman at Jacob's well raised secondary matters until the
Lord brought her to face her sin and Himself as the Messiah.

Do not let people dodge the real issue by raising a lot of
unimportant questions. Tell them to come to Christ and see
for themselves. He is in Himself the answer to all our problems. Whatever you may not understand, whatever puzzles
you, do not try to solve such things one by one. Come to
Him and He will dispel your doubts and you will say with
Nathanael, "Thou art the Son of God!"

## APRIL 3

### THE LESSON OF CHERITH: GOD'S PROVISION

*Get thee hence . . . and hide thyself by the brook
Cherith . . . and I have commanded the ravens to
feed thee there.* I KINGS 17:3, 4.

AT CHERITH ELIJAH learned the lesson of God's provision.
But Cherith was the place of God's provision because it was
the place of God's purpose. Elijah was in the place where
God told him to be. The ravens had been commanded to
feed him "there," not somewhere else, not just anywhere,
but "there." Where God guides He provides. He is responsible for our upkeep if we follow His directions. He is not
responsible for expenses not on His schedule. He does not
foot the bill when we leave His itinerary.

Sometimes God's arrangements are most unusual. Com-
manding the birds to feed a prophet is strange procedure.
And sometimes God sends us off to a brook when we think
we ought to be out in the thick of things. The need is so

75

great, the harvest so plenteous and the laborers so few that it looks like a waste of time to head for a brook. But God has His own pattern and plan, and He may want us by a mountain brook when we are all hot and bothered about getting into the heat of the battle. But it was at Cherith's brook that Elijah was made ready for Carmel's battle.

## APRIL 4

### THE LESSON OF CARMEL: GOD'S POWER

*The God that answereth by fire, let him be God.*
I Kings 18:24.

THE GREAT DAY on Carmel had all the elements of a mighty moving of God. There was the promise of showers of blessing (v. 1). There were the human efforts of Ahab and Obadiah to meet the need of the hour (2–16). There was God's man who was in a sense the troubler of Israel as the disturber of a false peace (17–20). There was the call to take a stand for God or Baal (21). There was the test of fire. Not "the God that answereth by finances or fame or feelings" but "by fire" (24). There was the repairing of broken altars (30). No wonder we read, "Then the fire of the Lord fell" (38), and "There is a sound of abundance of rain" (41).

Elijah prayed down both fire and water. We need both today. And we can have both. When the Fire of His Spirit falls from above, the floods of His blessing are sure to follow.

## APRIL 5

### THE LESSON OF THE CAVE: GOD'S PRESENCE

*And after the fire a still small voice.* I Kings 19:12.

IT WAS THE day after Carmel. The day after the big day can be a very bad day. From His baptism our Lord went to meet the devil. After the third heaven, Paul came to his thorn in the flesh.

But Elijah learned at the cave what he never learned on Carmel. We make so much these days of wind, fire, and earthquake, of the sensational and spectacular, of the dramatic demonstration on Carmel. We measure everything by "How big?" and "How loud?" God's voice in the cave was still and small. He does indeed speak in wind, fire, and quake, but those are occasional. Woe unto us if we are so deafened by the whirlwind that we cannot hear the whisper!

We are in great danger of going from one Carmel to another, living on excitement, mass meetings, and amazing demonstrations, that we need a session in the cave. Let us not deafen our ears to the quiet moving of God's Spirit in hundreds of humble hearts whose work of faith and labor of love will outlast anything on Carmel.

## APRIL 6

### PAUL'S CONFESSION

*But this I confess unto thee, that after the way which they call heresy, so worship I the God of my fathers.*
ACTS 24:14.

IN HIS MATCHLESS defense before Felix Paul is not ashamed to belong to the sect of the Nazarenes. He declares his position. He *asserts revelation behind him:* "Believing all things which are written in the law and in the prophets." He *anticipates the resurrection ahead of him:* "And have hope toward God . . . that there shall be a resurrection of the dead, both of the just and unjust." He *takes responsibility upon him:* "And herein do I exercise myself, to have always a conscience void of offense toward God and toward men."

It is possible to be very orthodox about revelation and the resurrection and yet to assume little responsibility for the way we live today. Paul lived *today* with *that day* always in mind. Faith in revelation past and hope in the resurrection to come should show up in godly exercise now.

## APRIL 7

### BOUGHT WITH AN INFINITE PRICE

*Forasmuch as ye know that ye were not redeemed with corruptible things, as silver and gold, from your vain conversation received by tradition from your fathers; but with the precious blood of Christ, as of a lamb without blemish and without spot.* I PETER 1:18, 19.

SALVATION IS FREE but not cheap. The gift of God cost God His Son and the Son His life. With His own precious blood He bought us in the market, bought us out of the market, bought us never to return to the market. We are not redeemed by anything we are or have or can do.

The New Testament theme is a glorious Three R's—Ruin, Redemption and Regeneration. There is a tendency today to make much of Christ as teacher and example, but when the Greeks came to see Him He spoke immediately of His death. Modern Greeks need the message of redemption by His blood.

It is also the incentive to consecration and service. Not the copying of an Example or following a Teacher, but because we are not our own, but are bought with a price—for *that* reason we are to glorify God in our body and spirit, which are God's.

78

## APRIL 8

### BESET BY INVISIBLE POWERS

*For we wrestle not against flesh and blood, but against principalities, against powers, against the rulers of the darkness of this world, against spiritual wickedness in high places.* EPHESIANS 6:12.

ANOTHER NEGATIVE-POSITIVE verse like yesterday's and this time we read that we are not up against flesh and blood these days. The devil is the prince of the power of the air, and he is assisted by legions of wicked spirits and evil angels. Never mind these wiseacres who talk of "outmoded ideas from ancient demonology." And do not turn all this over to psychiatrists. Any Christian who gets down to business in spiritual warfare soon finds himself against dark and sinister powers. Our Lord contended with that world during the days of His flesh and delivered men and women from it.

Satan and his legions are out to disable the body, deceive the mind, and discourage the spirit. Some he devours as a roaring lion. Some he leads astray as an angel of light. Others he besets as the accuser. He attacks through morals, through the mind, through moods.

Truly our souls need to be on their guard, for "ten thousand foes arise, the hosts of sin are pressing hard to draw us from the skies."

## APRIL 9

### BLESSED WITH AN INVISIBLE PRESENCE

*Not by might, nor by power, but by my spirit, saith the Lord of hosts.* ZECHARIAH 4:6.

HERE IS STILL another negative-positive that provides help in our dilemma. If there are hosts against us, there are also hosts on our side. The King of Syria sent a host against Elisha, but "behold, the mountain was full of horses and chariots round about Elisha." No wonder he assured his servant, "Fear not: for they that be with us are more than they that be with them."

If we are beset by an unseen foe, we are also befriended by an Unseen Friend. Great is our adversary but greater is our Ally. "The battle is the Lord's." If there are evil angels there are also good angels. "The angel of the Lord encampeth round about them that fear him, and delivereth them."

I noticed recently a repair shop operated by a man named Angel. His sign read, "Angel Service." I laughed and said, "I've had angel service for years. 'Are they not all ministering spirits sent forth to minister for them who shall be heirs of salvation?' "

Joshua, before the battle of Jericho, met the captain of the host of the Lord. The conquest of the hosts of evil depends on the Captain of the hosts of God. Before Jericho, meet Jesus!

## APRIL 10

### THE CHRIST OF EXPERIENCE

*Last of all he was seen of me also.* I CORINTHIANS 15:8.

IN THIS MARVELOUS and classic statement of the Gospel, Paul sets forth the *Christ of history:* "Christ died"; *the Christ of doctrine:* "Christ died for our sins"; *the Christ of the Scriptures:* "Christ died . . . was buried . . . and rose again the third day according to the Scriptures."

Then he moves further to declare *the Christ of experience,* the experience of others, to begin with. "He was seen of Cephas, then of the twelve, of above five hundred brethren at once, of James, of all the apostles." And finally he reaches a climax in *the Christ of his own experience:* "and last of all he was seen of me also."

It is possible to know Christ as a fact of history, of doctrine, of the Scriptures, of the experience of others, but it avails nothing if we cannot add, "Last of all he was seen of me also."

It was said of Thomas Chalmers that he had "an original experience of Jesus Christ." Have you seen Him for yourself?

## APRIL 11

### LORDS AND LEPERS

*A lord . . . said, Behold, if the Lord would make windows in heaven, might this thing be? . . . And there were four leprous men . . . and they said one to another, Why sit we here until we die?* II KINGS 7:2, 3.

THE "LORD" RIDICULED the idea that the siege of Samaria could be lifted and its famine relieved, but *The Lord* used lepers, of all people, to make the venture of desperation that brought deliverance. Truly, God keeps His secrets from the wise and prudent and reveals them unto babes. While King Jehoram and his experts and generals were at wit's end, God used the means least expected to turn the tide. It was not the wise, mighty, and noble who relieved Samaria but the base and despised. And while lords laughed, lepers demonstrated the power of God.

How often has the Almighty by-passed the high and mighty and confounded the experts, while some lowly soul on the verge of despair has put us all to shame by marching straight ahead in holy desperation to discover what the rest of us only debate! God proves Himself by raising up some nonentity who is willing to risk everything on a venture to show what God can do. While lords make light of it, lepers make history.

"Behold, if the Lord would make windows in heaven,

might this thing be?" "Prove me now herewith, saith *The Lord* of hosts, if I will not open you the windows of heaven." Which will you believe, "a lord" or *The Lord?*

## APRIL 12

### THREE-WAY FAITHFULNESS

*I have fought a good fight, I have finished my course, I have kept the faith.* II Timothy 4:7.

Paul was *faithful* to *the faith:* "I have kept the faith." Not only is faith itself a fight ("fight the good fight of faith"), but we are also to contend for the faith. So he was also *faithful to the fight:* "I have fought a good fight." And he was *faithful to the finish:* "I have finished my course."

Some are faithful to the faith, sound in belief, orthodox in doctrine, but are not faithful to the fight, do not contend for the faith. But Paul was "set for the defense of the Gospel," and because some have not been so minded, apostasy has taken over many a church and school. Still others are faithful to the faith and to the fight, but they give up the battle and do not endure unto the end; they are not faithful to the finish. We grow weary in well-doing all too soon. Paul did not soften up in old age and drift into that smiling tolerance which so many today think is a mark of broad-minded maturity.

We are in deep need of three-way faithfulness, to the faith, to the fight, to the finish.

## APRIL 13

### "SUPPOSING"

*But they, supposing him to have been in the company, went a day's journey.* Luke 2:44.

Joseph and mary supposed Jesus was with them when He was not. How many religious groups and movements run

82

on for years long after Jesus has dropped out from the procession!

How many churches still carry on their program, their Sunday-by-Sunday uprisings and downsittings and yet, like Samson, wist not that the Spirit of the Lord has departed! And all because so many of us go on many a day's journey after we have left Jesus far behind, so far as the conscious sense of His presence and blessing is concerned. We sing the same songs, say the same prayers, give the same testimonies, but men see Him not in their lives because His presence is only a supposition.

It will not do to proceed on a supposition. We must make sure of Jesus or we travel in vain. Nothing is so futile as religious activity that only imagines the Lord's presence. We might well inquire, "Is the Lord among us or not?" It is wrong to doubt His presence when we may be sure of it, but it is foolish to imagine His presence when there is proper occasion to doubt it.

## APRIL 14

### PRAYER IS NOT ENOUGH

*If my people, which are called by my name, shall humble themselves, and pray, and seek my face, and turn from their wicked ways; then will I hear from heaven, and will forgive their sin, and will heal their land.*
II Chronicles 7:14.

It will readily be seen here that God requires four things, not just one. And He will not settle for a fourth of what He requires. If we are going to use this verse let us use all of it. Sometimes we make it sound as though a prayer meeting alone were sufficient to produce a revival. God has said more here than "pray."

We are to humble ourselves—not pray for humility, but

humble ourselves, "as a little child" (Mt. 18:4), "in the sight of the Lord" (Jas. 4:10), "under the mighty hand of God" (I Pt. 5:6). We are to seek God's face, His favor, the smile of His approval. "When thou saidst, Seek ye my face, my heart said unto thee, Thy face, Lord, will I seek" (Ps. 27:8). Is that what your heart says?

And we are to turn from our wicked ways. That fourth note is rather subdued these days. "He that covereth his sins shall not prosper: but whoso confesseth and forsaketh them shall have mercy" (Prov. 28:13).

Praying is not enough if God requires more. And in this sadly misused text He certainly does!

## APRIL 15

### THE GIFT AND THE GIVER

*Bring no more vain oblations.* ISAIAH 1:13.
*The churches of Macedonia . . . first gave their own selves to the Lord.* II CORINTHIANS 8:1, 5.

WHAT GOD WANTS is not yours but you. Self, service, substance—that is the Divine order. Ananias and Sapphira not only did not give all they had, they never gave themselves.

Prebendary Webb-Peploe used to say, "Sometimes I buy gifts for my wife. I fear that my choices are often very poor but she accepts them with good grace because she knows that before I ever gave her gifts I gave her my heart."

Alas, there are heartbroken wives whose husbands bring flowers and finery but who have never really given their hearts' love. And how God is grieved when we bring Him vain oblations! A check on the collection plate means nothing to Him if we withhold ourselves. The little boy who dropped into the offering basket a slip of paper bearing the words, "I give myself," had the right idea.

The Macedonians started right. They gave themselves. When God gets you He will get yours. You have to be more than a "check-book Christian." For "the gift without the giver is bare."

## "WE HAVE FELLOWSHIP"

*We have fellowship . . .* I JOHN 1:7.

PRECIOUS INDEED IS the fellowship of those whose citizenship is in heaven. We have *fellowship with the Saviour:* "God is faithful by whom ye were called unto the fellowship of his Son Jesus Christ" (I Cor. 1:9). We have *the fellowship of the Spirit* (Phil. 2:1). There is *the fellowship of His sufferings* (Phil. 3:10). We enjoy *the fellowship of the Saints* (I John 1:7; Acts 2:42). There is *the fellowship of service:* "the fellowship of ministering to the saints" (II Cor. 8:4).

But there is also a *fellowship of Satan:* "Have no fellowship with the unfruitful works of darkness, but rather reprove them" (Eph. 5:11). "If we say we have fellowship with him, and walk in darkness, we lie and do not the truth" (I John 1:6). "What fellowship hath righteousness with unrighteousness?" (II Cor. 6:14).

We cannot have a *heavenly* fellowship if we allow a *hindering* fellowship. "Little children, keep yourselves from idols" (I John 5:21).

## CARNALITIES AND SPIRITUALITIES

*Ye are yet carnal.* I CORINTHIANS 3:3.
*Now concerning spiritual gifts . . .* I CORINTHIANS 12:1.

DR. G. CAMPBELL MORGAN has pointed out that Paul in First Corinthians begins with the carnalities and then moves in the latter part of the book to the spiritualities. In doing so he runs counter to the modern policy of "accentuating the positive" and not dealing with sins in the church on the premise that if we emphasize love the problems in the church will vanish. If the modern approach is correct, then Paul should have begun with the thirteenth chapter of this epistle. Instead, he dealt with definite sins, following pet preachers, schisms, immorality, disorders at the Lord's table. Then he was ready to consider spiritual gifts, preach on love and the resurrection—and even take a collection!

In Christian experience, we cannot move on to deeper things until sin has been faced in our lives. Nor can we in the church. Joshua on his face was no substitute for cleansing the camp from Achan, and prayer meetings cannot compensate for not getting rid of golden wedges and all accursed things.

We must deal with our carnalities if we desire the spiritualities.

## APRIL 18

### BREAD IN THE WILDERNESS

*From whence can a man satisfy these men with bread here in the wilderness.* MARK 8:4.

"BREAD IN THE wilderness" sounds as incongruous as "streams in the desert." Remember the Old Testament complaint, "Can God furnish a table in the wilderness?" (Ps. 78:19). Indeed, no man could meet such an emergency, but our Lord did. With the five thousand, the miracle moved in three stages. There was *a lack of bread.* Jesus asked Philip, "Whence shall we buy bread that these may eat?" but He knew what He would do, as He always knew. Philip surmised that two hundred pennyworth of bread would not be enough. We are always "making an estimate," like Philip, but we leave out the supernatural.

There was *a little bread*. Five loaves and two fishes amount to little, either in quantity or quality, but "little is much if God is in it." So a little bread became *a lot of bread*. There was a surplus of twelve basketfuls. God never deals niggardly. If each disciple gathered a basket full he had more than he started with!

And all because "there is a lad here." His little in Jesus' hands became a lot. No man can furnish a table in the wilderness, but Jesus and a boy can do it.

<br>

**APRIL 19**

**CHRIST IS "IT"**

*We preach not ourselves, but Christ Jesus the Lord.*
II Corinthians 4:5.

BY DIVERSE PATHS and through varying experiences God's men through the ages have arrived at the simple conclusion that what matters is Christ Himself, in doctrine, in experience, in preaching. We assume that everybody knows this, but here is our weakness. We assent to it theoretically, but we take it for granted and what we take for granted we never take seriously. We assume it but we ought to assert it. What we take as a matter of course we should be shouting from the housetops.

My own personal experience, reached through several stages, has arrived at the conviction with which I should have started—that the issue is simply Christ Himself. Familiar? Yes, but do we need anything so much these days as to familiarize ourselves with the familiar?

It is so perilously easy to preach less than Christ Himself —our own experience, a pet doctrine; a partial, fragmentary Gospel; a phase of Christ, a facet of His character instead of Himself, in whom all is included. This is "It," "Christ Jesus the Lord"—Messiah, Mediator, Master.

## APRIL 20

### THE ALL-INCLUSIVE LOYALTY

*Married to another . . . to him who is raised from the dead, that we should bring forth fruit unto God.*
ROMANS 7:4.

IF THE ISSUE is Christ, then surely for us the issue is just to be Christians. A Christian is a *Christ-ian,* and his supreme loyalty is to Christ. Better than that, his loyalty to Christ is all-inclusive; it comprehends all lesser devotions.

That does not exclude the lesser loyaties. A man is a better citizen of his country if he is faithful to his own family. A man is a better member of the whole household of faith if he is loyal to his own local church and religious group.

But when the lesser loyalty transcends the greater, then there is trouble. There is a place for political parties, but any man who puts party above the country and plays cheap politics in an hour of peril is a traitor. A man should be first an American before he is a Democrat or Republican. There is a place for local and group loyalty in the church, but a man who cannot, and will not, be a Christian first is a traitor to Jesus Christ.

We are married to Christ. A wife takes her husband's name, and a true wife will make all other human loyalties subservient to that. A Christian bears the name of Christ, and his loyalty to Christ includes and glorifies all other relationships. Christ does not merely come first, He is Alpha and Omega, and includes the alphabet of all our interests and affections.

## THREE-WAY CHRISTIANS

*And* believers *were the more added to the Lord.* ACTS
5:14.
*If ye continue in my word, then are ye my disciples
indeed.* JOHN 8:31.
*Ye shall be witnesses unto me.* ACTS 1:8.

WHAT IS A New Testament Christian? He is a heart-believer
in a crucified and risen Saviour and Lord. But our churches
are filled with believers who do not continue in His Word
and so are poor disciples. Salvation is free—not cheap—
and we have only to trust Christ to be believers. But discipleship calls for all we are and have.

We have unwittingly created an artificial distinction between trusting Christ as Saviour and obeying Him as Lord.
The New Testament recognizes no such false compartments
of experience. "Believe on the LORD Jesus Christ," said
Paul to the jailer. No man can be a Christian by knowingly
and wilfully taking Christ on the installment plan, as
Saviour now, as Lord later.

And we are all His witnesses, witnesses unto Him (Acts
1:8) and witnesses to the truth about Him (Lk. 24:48). We
are witnesses of His death and resurrection in our own experience and witnesses to Him in testimony. By life and
lip we declare Him; we know Him and make Him known.


## APRIL 22

### BETTER CHRISTIANS

*Grow in grace, and in the knowledge of our Lord and
Saviour Jesus Christ.* II PETER 3:18.

THE FIRST BUSINESS of a Christian is to become a better
Christian, to know Christ better, to decrease that He may

increase. "That I may know him" was Paul's supreme ambition.

It is possible to major on the negative side of this matter on separation alone or to stress solely the positive aspect in the victorious life, or Spirit-filled life, so that we develop a fad. The Christian life is Christ Himself. There is the positive, "Put ye on the Lord Jesus Christ" and the negative, "Make not provision for the flesh, to fulfil the lusts thereof," and it is all simply more of Christ and less of self.

Here is a weak spot today. For all our religious wheels within wheels, we have no time for the cultivation of our souls, no time to know Christ better. How does He become more real? "He that hath my commandments, and keepeth them, he it is that loveth me: and he that loveth me shall be loved of my Father, and I will love him, *and will manifest myself to him*" (Jno. 14:21). He makes Himself real to the obedient disciple. And the obedient disciple is daily a better Christian than he was the day before.


## APRIL 23

### THE PERFECTING OF THE SAINTS

*For the perfecting of the saints.* EPHESIANS 4:12.

IT IS ALSO the business of every believer to help other Christians to become better Christians. If a brother be overtaken in a fault we are to pray for him, not persecute him. Jesus was out to restore backsliding Peter, to fire him up—not fire him out. Peter was marked "Special"; "Go tell his disciples *and Peter.*"

The New Testament abounds in instructions to love one another, exhort one another, comfort one another, forgive one another, prefer one another, provoke one another to love and good works. We provoke one another, but not to love and good works!

The gifts of our Lord to the church, apostles, prophets,

evangelists, pastors and teachers, are not for display but "for the perfecting of the saints, for the work of the ministry, for the edifying of the body of Christ: *till we all come in the unity of the faith, and of the knowledge of the Son of God.*" To know Him ourselves and to help others to know Him better!

And as we help in the perfecting of others we are perfected ourselves. Working on ourselves all the time produces a warped saint. Our best improvement comes roundabout, indirectly, as we help one another along.

## APRIL 24

### GATHERERS

*He that is not with me is against me; and he that gathereth not with me scattereth abroad.* MATTHEW 12:30.

OUR LORD HERE joins position with practice. We are first with Him—not just for Him—and out of that grows duty: we gather with Him. "Follow me and I will make you fishers of men"—there again He joins relationship with results, fellowship with fruitfulness: "Abide in me . . . much fruit."

Our business is to become better Christians ourselves, help others to be better Christians, and win still others to become Christians. It grows naturally out of being a believer and disciple that one should also be a witness. Andrew did not have to take a study course in soul-winning to send him after his brother Peter, nor did Philip have to be urged during an annual "revival" before he did "personal work" with Nathanael.

When anything good comes our way we usually tell it. Strange that the greatest good tidings of all should find us holding our peace. Maybe we have just become canvassers looking for "members" instead of gatherers looking for souls.

91

## APRIL 25

### BACK TO ANTIOCH

*The disciples were called Christians first in Antioch.*
Acts 11:26.

IN THIS MODERN Babel we would do well to get back to Antioch again. Well might some "Jesus man" call us back to Christ Himself and the glorious privilege of being "just Christians."

The traveler has been lost in the baggage. We are so cluttered with all the things that go with the Christian life that we can hardly identify the Christian. We become so identified with a fragment of the truth or a segment of the church that it is hard for people to think of us as representatives of Christ Himself.

Through the ages men have risen who sought to recapture the simplicity of New Testament Christianity. But the simple soon becomes complex, and they end with another denomination, the very thing they started out to get away from. There is a man, a movement, a machine, and a monument!

No, the solution does not lie in that direction. A man may continue in the same set-up, but he can transcend it and even restore to it the luster it once had by being a real New Testament Christian first of all.

## APRIL 26

### "STRENGTHEN THY STAKES"

*Lengthen thy cords, and strengthen thy stakes.* ISAIAH 54:2.

IF WE ARE going to lengthen our cords we had better strengthen our stakes. The church today is intent on expanding borders and taking in more territory. That is good if along with it we strengthen what we have. Otherwise, we gain width at the expense of depth and become shallow. The Christian and the church need an intensive as well as an extensive ministry. Vast ingatherings of believers bring peril if we do not teach, indoctrinate, build up in the faith. To use A. J. Gordon's illustration, the average church is often like a congested lung with only a few cells doing the breathing. There is usually a faithful nucleus surrounded by a mass of nominal Christians.

While we extend the borders of our tent, we had better check the center pole. We must fix the point of our compass properly before we describe our circles. We are in tremendous need of a ministry to strengthen our stakes that we may go further as we go deeper.

## APRIL 27

### "DAILY"

*And they, continuing daily. . . . And the Lord added to the church daily such as should be saved.* ACTS 2:46,47.

THE NEW TESTAMENT does not abound in instruction as to what we now call "personal work" and "soul-winning." The epistles indoctrinate and exhort as to Christian growth, and it seems to be assumed that a normal Christian will by life and lip win others.

Nowadays we drive and plan and put on courses galore trying to get Christians to do what should be their natural practice, not only with regard to reaching the lost, but with regard to church attendance, tithing, missions, and all other phases of service. All of this should be the spontaneous expression of our love for Christ and others.

The Early Church continued *daily* in fellowship and faithfulness, and the Lord added *daily* in fruitfulness. What we labor and sweat to produce is a natural consequence in the Scriptures. It is high time we majored on the conditions

93

that produce the results we seek. A church in faith and fellowship will be faithful and fruitful. Which brings it, of course, to the door of each of us. If we follow Him *daily* He will make us fishers of men *daily*.

## APRIL 28

### TIDINGS OR TUMULT?

*Thou hast no tidings ready? . . . I saw a great tumult.*
II SAMUEL 18:22, 29.

AHIMAAZ WANTED TO run when he had nothing to report. Consequently, he could only say, "I saw a great tumult." The messenger who runs too soon in the ministry has only a tempest in his head and in his heart.

Smitten as we are today with the delusion that we are doing most business when we are busiest, we need to learn John Wesley's maxim, "I do not have time to be in a hurry." God is saying to some of us, "Stand thou still awhile that I may shew thee the Word of God." We are not to wear out or to rust out, but to live out, and God has as much to say about being still as about being busy. In this age of aspirin and angina a preacher may have to offend somebody in order to eliminate enough nonessentials to make time to get his tidings ready.

Otherwise, he will have seen only a tumult, and this poor world needs no more tumults.

## APRIL 29

### RESTING AND ROUSING

*I will give you rest.* MATTHEW 11:28.
*Rise, let us be going.* MATTHEW 26:46.

HE RESTS US and He rouses us. This nervous age keeps going with pills to put it to sleep and pills to keep it awake. From sedative to stimulant our generation lives by shots in the arm. We both rest and rouse our jaded selves artificially.

But all we need for both purposes is found in Jesus. He gives us His peace. "Rest in the Lord" is God's prescription. "Entered Into Rest" should not be limited to epitaphs on tombstones. We can enter into His rest any time we cease from our own feverish works and rest in His finished work.

And He rouses us. "Be not drunk with wine wherein is excess, but be filled with the Spirit." There you have the world's false stimulant and the Divine stirring of the Spirit. "Stir up the gift of God" means kindling the Fire within us, although the coals may be covered with ashes. Alas, "there is none that stirreth up himself to take hold of God."

Whether you need resting or rousing, He does both. But we co-operate as we rest in Him or rouse ourselves to do His bidding.

## APRIL 30

### CAN YOU READ SIGNS?

*O ye hypocrites, ye can discern the face of the sky; but can ye not discern the signs of the times?* MATTHEW 16:3.

WE MUST HAVE another sort of discernment if, like the children of Issachar, we are to have understanding of the times to know what Israel ought to do. If we can escape from all the wrangling and simply read our New Testaments, we can recover a clear view of what lies ahead: civilization a decaying carcass awaiting the vultures, anarchy in the world, apostasy in the professing church, apathy even among true believers. Beyond that, the final showdown between Christ and Antichrist, God who became man and the man who will claim to be God; Armageddon, the final world conflict, and the Appearing of our Lord.

There is no denying that the early Christians, while they lived and learned, also looked for Jesus to return any day. But Constantine became a professed believer and Augustine envisioned his City of God, and since then we have tried to build here the Kingdom instead of bringing back the King.

And do not forget that the man who says there are no "signs" is himself a sign! (II Pt. 3:3, 4).

## MAY I

### "LET IT BEGIN IN ME"

*If my people . . . shall humble* themselves . . . *then will I . . .* II Chronicles 7:14.

In revival God begins with His own people, and His people begin with *themselves* . . . "humble *themselves*" . . . "turn from *their* wicked ways." It is subjective: they humble themselves and turn from sin. It is objective: they pray and seek God's face. After David has his joy restored, then he teaches transgressors God's ways, and sinners are converted. David does not go out visiting prospects and canvassing sinners until he has dealt with himself.

Getting church members busy with other duties in a revival before they themselves have repented defeats the whole purpose of revival. "Search *me*, O God, and know *my* heart, try *me* and know *my* thoughts: and see if there be any wicked way in *me*, and lead *me* in the way everlasting." "Lord, send a revival and let it begin in *me*"—well, that is where it must begin. Not in absentee church members but in us who are present on Sunday morning and assume that we are all right and so merely make plans to get someone else revived.

96

## MAY 2

### PLEASURES .... SEASONAL AND PERENNIAL

*The pleasures of sin* for a season. HEBREWS 11:25.
*At thy right hand there are pleasures forevermore.*
PSALM 16:17.

MOSES CHOSE THE imperishable. He had his eye on Him who is invisible. No wonder that he did the impossible! Sin's pleasures are only *for a season*. "She that liveth in pleasure is dead while she liveth." "For all that is in the world, the lust of the flesh, and the lust of the eyes and the pride of life, is not of the Father, but is of the world. *And the world passeth away* and the lust thereof: but he that doeth the will of God *abideth forever.*"

God's pleasures are perennial. This poor age loves the temporal. It lives from one passing fancy to another. Today's hit is forgotten tomorrow. Everything is *for a season.* Its shows, its styles, bear the label *"this season."* The man who lives in God is never out of season. "The fashion of this world passeth away," but he is not of this world.

Do you have the "joy that *remains*"?


## MAY 3

### GOD'S CURE FOR IGNORANCE

*I would not have you ignorant* . . . ROMANS 11:25; I
CORINTHIANS 10:1; II CORINTHIANS 1:8; I THESSA-
LONIANS 4:13; II PETER 3:8.

THE OUTSTANDING CHARACTERISTIC of this intellectual age, believe it or not, is ignorance. We do err, not knowing the Scriptures or the power of God (Mt. 22:29).

*The world does not know its peril*, like those of Noah's day who ate and drank, married and gave in marriage *and knew not* (Mt. 24:39). *The church does not know its need.* It is like Laodicea, that boasted it was rich and increased

97

with goods and had need of nothing *and knew not* that it was wretched, miserable, poor, blind and naked (Rev. 3: 17). *The sinner does not know the saviour.* Jesus said to the woman at Jacob's well, "If thou knewest the gift of God and *who* it is that saith to thee, Give me to drink . . ." (Jno. 4:10).

*And Christians do not know the Lord.* "Have I been so long time with you, and yet thou hast not known me, Philip?" was our Lord's pointed question to His dull disciple (Jno. 14:9). We know Him so poorly, we are so ignorant of the power of His resurrection and the fellowship of His sufferings.

Ignorance unbounded! And the cure is to know God and Jesus Christ whom He has sent (Jno. 17:3).

## MAY 4

### LET IT SHINE!

*Let your light so shine before men, that they may see your good works, and glorify your Father which is in heaven.* MATTHEW 5:16.

SOME HIDE THEIR light under bushel or bed (Mk. 4:21; Lk. 8:16), being busy or lazy, so that it fails to shine. Some go to the other extreme, like the Pharisees (Mt. 6:1, 2, 16), who wanted to impress people with their piety. It is not a glare but a glow, and we are simply to let it shine. Some saints remind us of a man with a high-powered flashlight trying to dazzle people with a blinding display. God prefers stars to comets. His figure is a candle, not a firecracker.

Between the saints who hide their light and those who display it we have hard going these days. We learn more and more to appreciate those who just let it shine. We are too aware of the "men" in our text and not aware enough of our Father. Our sole business is to glorify Him and so let our light shine that others will glorify Him too.

## NO OFFENSE, NO EFFECT

*God forbid that I should glory save in the cross of our
Lord Jesus Christ.* GALATIANS 6:14.

WE NEED *men of the cross*, with the *message of the cross*
bearing the *marks of the cross*.

Paul was a MAN *of the cross*. He gloried in it. "I am
crucified with Christ" (Gal. 2:20). With him it was not a
theory but an experience. His *message was the cross*. "I determined not to know anything among you save Jesus
Christ, and him crucified" (I Cor. 2:2). He bore the *marks
of the cross:* "I bear in my body the marks of the Lord
Jesus" (Gal. 6:17).

We are hearing a new version of Christianity that avoids
all this. It is not foolishness to the world and it is without
offense. It involves no crucifixion of self, it presents no
bleeding Saviour, it offers medals instead of scars. But if
any man or an angel preach a crossless Christ let him be
accursed. For such a Christ is without offense and without
effect.

## ASHAMED TO BLUSH

*O my God, I am ashamed and blush to lift up my face
to thee, my God: for our iniquities are increased over
our head, and our trespass is grown up unto the heavens.* EZRA 9:6.

JEREMIAH LAMENTED IN a verse found twice in his book
(6:15; 8:12) that his generation knew no shame and could
not blush. He declared that God's blessing had been with-
held because they refused to be ashamed (3:3). Ezra is
ashamed and blushes for the sins of his people.

People used to blush when they were ashamed. Now they are ashamed if they blush. Modesty has disappeared and a brazen generation with no fear of God before its eyes mocks at sin. There is no revival, because even God's people will not humble themselves in sorrow for sin. Nothing is more needed than a sense of shame.

God give us Ezras and Jeremiahs who are ashamed and blush for their day and generation instead of defending it, lightly regarding the hurt of the land, saying, "Peace," when there is no peace. We are so fond of being called tolerant and broad-minded that we wink at sin when we ought to weep.


## MAY 7

### CONFIDENCE AND COMMITTAL

*I know whom I have believed, and am persuaded that he is able to keep that which I have committed unto him against that day.* II TIMOTHY 1:12.

PAUL'S CONFIDENCE IN Christ led to committal. In the home town of my boyhood days we had two banks. I had confidence in both, but committed my money to only one. A man might have utmost confidence in a bank but it will not keep his money until he deposits it. Paul made the deposit.

The housewife who, when told to endorse a check, wrote, "I heartily endorse this check," was not unlike some of us in spiritual matters. We endorse the Bible as God's Word and Jesus as God's Son, but we do not actually "sign our name," we do not make it personal. We believe, but we do not commit all we are and have to it.

Have you made the deposit? He will keep what you commit. Be sure your faith is confidence plus committal.

## MAY 8

### THE THREE "CANNOTS"

*He cannot be my disciple.* LUKE 14:26, 27, 33.

IF WE HATE not family and even our own lives; if we bear not our cross and come after Him; if we forsake not all that we have, we cannot be His disciples. He does not say we will be poor disciples, He says we cannot be His disciples at all. Tone it down all you will, the cleverest exegesis cannot do much with this threefold test. Why is it that we are so silent on such texts today? We have let down the bars and we take all comers. Our catch-all invitations gather in a motley mixture, a mixed multitude. Screen them with these three "cannots" and see how much wheat is left when the chaff is gone!

These words were spoken to a great multitude. We would be flattered by such a following, but our Lord immediately thinned His crowd. Is it not time we whittled down Gideon's unwieldy band to a hard core of effectives? But, alas, this is the day of statistics, and we must make a good showing on the books.

## MAY 9

### "WILL YE ALSO GO AWAY?"

*Will ye also go away?* JOHN 6:67.

AS RECORDED IN the sixth chapter of John, Jesus lost His crowd. And if today we really faced the impact of that sermon He preached on the Bread of Life would not most of us say, "This is an hard saying; who can hear it?" "Except ye eat the flesh of the Son of man, and drink his blood, ye have no life in you." How many, think you, of our present comfortable Sunday-morning churchgoers are ready for that?

The appropriation of Christ our Life by faith—what strange doctrine that is to the average soul! Men follow for loaves and fishes, but they walk out on Him when they discover what He really means. This sort of preaching still will thin out congregations. "This is an hard saying"—we will go elsewhere and hear book reviews.

"Christ our Life"—preach that and you will lose the crowd, but you will have the Irreducible Minimum who say with Peter, "Lord, to whom shall we go? Thou hast the words of eternal life. And we believe and are sure that thou art that Christ, the Son of the living God."

## MAY 10

### "HINDER ME NOT"

*Hinder me not, seeing the Lord hath prospered my way.* GENESIS 24:56.

ABRAHAM'S SERVANT NEEDED plenty of guidance. A man looking for a wife for himself needs all the illumination he can get, but this servant was looking for a wife for some-body else! Being in the way, as he put it, the Lord led him and he found the right girl. Now the subtle temptation to tarry awhile arises. It looks innocent enough, but he is on his guard. It is dangerous to linger. He will be on his journey. "Hinder me not, seeing the Lord hath prospered my way."

We are often faced with the tempter's suggestion to tarry, linger awhile, take it easy. But if the Lord has pros-pered our way we had better be going. Layovers at Satan's suggestion become layoffs, and we fail of our mission. The diligent servant who is about his master's business will take no holiday when he should be up and about and on his way home.

It would have been pleasant to enjoy the hospitality of Rebekah's kinfolk and they meant well, no doubt. But the most innocent and well-intentioned can spell havoc with God's timetable.

"Rise, let us be going."


## MAY 11

### HIS JOY

*These things have I spoke unto you, that my joy might remain in you, and that your joy might be full.* JOHN 15:11.

THE JOY OF the Lord is not the natural exuberance of youth. It is not ordinary human enthusiasm. It is not the exhilaration caused by favorable happenings and circumstances. It is not the emotion whipped up by high-pressure hilarity. All these may have their place, but the joy Jesus gives is different. It outlasts youth. It is more than human, it is Divine. It is present, no matter what happens. It is not worked up, it comes down. It comes from a Man of Sorrows acquainted with grief. It lasts, it remains. And it is full, not partial.

Because of our shallow living we know little of this joy, so we work hard trying to pump up a substitute. How much of our religious life today runs on the same stimulus that a cheer leader works up before a ball game! But it is a poor substitute, it has a hollow ring and it gives out when we need help most.

Make His joy your joy!

## MAY 12

### GREEKS TO SEE JESUS

*Except a corn of wheat fall into the ground and die, it abideth alone: but if it die, it bringeth forth much fruit.* JOHN 12:24.

THIS WAS A momentous occasion. Some Greeks wanted to see Jesus. Philip and Andrew reported it to the Master. There is no record that He received these Greeks. Maybe they came out of curiosity, anxious to hear a great teacher or see Him perform a miracle. Anyway, Jesus made it clear that His was the way of death and a cross, not earthly popularity, and that we must die to live.

Today we are in danger of being misled by some Greeks who would see Jesus. Many would be glad to have the joy and peace that He gives, would copy Him as a teacher and leader. But they do not want the cross. They resent Calvary, nor do they want to deny self, take up their cross, and lose their lives to find them. Jesus receives no Greeks except by the way which was, and is, to them "foolishness."

## MAY 13

### "THERE FAILED NOT OUGHT"

*There failed not ought of any good thing which the Lord had spoken unto the house of Israel; all came to pass.* JOSHUA 21:45.

IN RECOUNTING THE goodness of God to Israel, Joshua tells us that the Lord gave them the Promised Land just as He had said He would. Joshua repeats it in an address to the people (23:14). Solomon said it in like fashion years later (I Kgs. 8:56).

If you will survey the path already trod you will say so too. "There hath failed not ought of any good thing God has spoken . . . all came to pass." If it hasn't, it will. He which hath begun a good work in us will finish it. He will perfect that which concerneth us.

It ought to fill our hearts wtih thanksgiving, our eyes with tears and our lips with praise, for "the goodness of God leadeth to repentance."

"There failed not ought . . ." But how we have failed Him!

## MAY 14

### "FOOLISHNESS" STILL

*The preaching of the cross is to them that perish foolishness.* I CORINTHIANS 1:18.

IT WAS "FOOLISHNESS" to the world then and it still is. Religion is very popular today and some are misled by that fact. A scared and desperate generation, having tried all else, is considering religion. But they do not want the preaching of the cross. Jesus the Example and Teacher maybe, Christianity as a lovely philosophy, but not a crucified Saviour. That is still "foolishness" to this age and ever will be.

And to most church members the counterpart of Christ's death for our sin, our death with Him and resurrection to walk with Him in newness of life, is just as unpopular. Call upon the average congregation to live out Romans 6, with its "reckon," "yield," and "obey," and you will hear few "amens."

The preaching of the cross in its meaning for sinner and saint is still "foolishness" to sinners and distasteful to not a few saints.

## MAY 15

### HEAT AND LIGHT

*He was a burning and a shining light.* JOHN 5:35.

SO SPAKE OUR Lord of John the Baptist. The Forerunner had both heat and light. It is a combination not always found in one personality. Some saints have heat aplenty, but they need light, wisdom, guidance. Some have light, but it is cold; there is no fire, no warmth. Someone has said, "Youth has fire without light and age has light without fire."

It is hard to tell which has done most harm, hotheaded ignorance or cold-hearted knowledge. The wild street preacher, screaming and tearing his hair, needs to burn less and shine more. The cold, intellectual preacher in stiff Sunday-morning formalism needs to shine less and burn more.

John the Baptist burned and shone. "Stir up the gift of God . . ." "Let your light so shine . . ." Give us more witnesses with both heat and light!

## MAY 16

### EATING THE COOK BOOK

*Except ye eat of the flesh of the Son of man, and drink his blood, ye have no life in you.* JOHN 6:53.

MANY DEAR PEOPLE have a lovely doctrine or theory of the victorious life or the indwelling Christ or the Spirit-filled life, and they try to live on their theory, but they do not feed on Christ. They are like a man trying to live on a cookbook instead of food, chewing on a seed catalogue instead of on vegetables. They may be very orthodox Bible students, but they do not chew and digest the words which are spirit and life.

It is tragic to go through our days making Christ the

106

subject of our study but not the sustenance of our souls. It is not the Word hid in the head but in the heart that keeps from sin. To appropriate Christ Himself, the Bread of Life, is to live by faith and grow. You can starve reading books on bread. You can search the Scriptures and not come to Him for life.

## MAY 17

### "WHO'S WHO?"

*"Who am I?"*
*I AM THAT I AM.* Exodus 3:11,14.

On "THE BACKSIDE of the desert" Moses came to "the mountain of God." When God called him to his mighty task Moses was first taken up with his own insufficiency—"Who am I?" But God made it clear that what mattered was not what Moses was but who God is: "I Am That I Am."

Jeremiah had the same fear as Moses: "I am but a child." God corrected him: "Say not, I am a child. . . . I am with thee to deliver thee." "Who is sufficient for these things?" asked Paul, and then he moved on to declare, "Our sufficiency is of God."

Moses started with ·"Who am I?" but soon asked God, "Who are you?" It is well for a man to know his own inadequacy, but woe unto him if he stop there. Let him move on to meet God and find Him sufficient.

It is not a matter of who I am but of who He is.

## MAY 18

### "BACKSIDE OF THE DESERT"

*And he led the flock to the backside of the desert, and came to the mountain of God.* Exodus 3:1.

Consider again where Moses met God at the end of his forty-year postgraduate course in Midian. In the unlikeliest place and at the unlikeliest time God brings us to the Great Moment. Moses, the adopted son of Pharaoh's daughter, brought up in the courts of Egypt, had known more glamorous days than now, a shepherd in a desert. But the big day and the hallowed spot, however drab and ordinary on calendar or map, are the time and place when we meet God and do business with Him.

There may not be even a burning bush. And God may not reward with an immediate evidence of His presence and power. But the man who has come to God honestly and simply and humbly, with no reservations, offering a willing heart, feeling or no feeling, that man has reached his Horeb, and though he be on the backside of a desert, he is also at the mountain of God.

## MAY 19

### NO OPTION

*Ye are not your own . . . for ye are bought with a price: therefore glorify God in your body, and in your spirit, which are God's.* I CORINTHIANS 6:19, 20.

IT HAS BEEN said that becoming a Christian is optional, but after we become Christians we have no option, we are to obey. Most church members are strangely ignorant of that. We go on living as though we were our own and had paid for our redemption. But we are not owners of anything, we are stewards of everything we are and have. And it is required of stewards that they be faithful. It is required of servants that they serve. It is required of soldiers that they obey. And every Christian is a steward, a servant, and a soldier.

We have no right to anything, we are bought and paid for

by the blood of Christ. We are His property. It is not for us lightly to choose what we shall give or withhold. We belong to Another and He has the say-so.

What a long way we are from realizing this on Sunday morning, when we have to be begged and besought to give God a tip! To withhold one thing is theft, for everything is His!

## MAY 20

### RICH AND HEALTHY

*Beloved, I wish above all things that thou mayest prosper and be in health, even as thy soul prospereth.*
III JOHN 2.

JOHN IS NOT conditioning Gaius' prosperity and health on the state of his soul, but rather is assuming his soul's prosperity as a fact. Nevertheless, it is true that God wants no man to be richer than his soul, and the spiritual condition is the true gauge of a man's real success. No man with a sick soul is really prosperous. Even the medical world stresses as never before the connection between health and religion.

Prosperity, health, and spirituality are here joined, and well they may be. The man who is right with God and men is in a fair way to being in good health. Even if the outer man decay, the inner man is renewed from day to day. And a new body is guaranteed as part of his salvation. And prosperity is assured, for whatsoever the righteous man doeth shall prosper. The man who is rich toward God is truly rich, and he who is healthy in his soul is truly healthy. Along with it, we shall have such material prosperity and physical health as we need—and why should we want more?

## ENDLESS QUEST

*Ever learning, and never able to come to a knowledge
of the truth.* II TIMOTHY 3:7.

WHEN WE COME to a decision about a spiritual matter,
Satan would worry us and keep us in fear that perhaps we
did not do right. But never to come to a decision is still
worse unbelief than to come with weak faith. To settle a
matter as best one knows how in accordance with Scripture, even though one's cry is, "Lord, I believe; help thou
mine unbelief," is certainly nearer the truth than not to
come at all. Christ will receive all who come. In the Gospels
they simply came, and He commended their faith when
they thought they had little.

What pleases God is faith, and the weakest faith is better
than no faith. Faith does not look at itself. One does not
see sight by closing his eyes and looking around on the inside of his head. He looks at something, and what he sees
confirms the fact that he has sight. Looking unto Jesus we
find that He meets our need and proves that we have faith.

"Ever learning" is not the way to truth. Look and live
and learn as you go.

## CALL TO AMERICA

*Hear the word of the Lord.* ISAIAH 1:10.

WE NEED TO recover Isaiah's thundering call from the moth-
balls where we have relegated it. The first chapter could be
proclaimed, with a few names changed, to America and be
strictly up to date. Surely our people "doth not consider."

Surely the moral putrefaction Isaiah portrayed (vs. 5, 6) smells just as bad in our land. And God hates our Sunday-morning religion without reality as much as He despised the sham formalities of Judah (vs. 11–15). Religion is popular nowadays, but we will not put away evil and learn to do well (vs. 16, 17). We want a religion that involves no break with the world, the flesh, and the devil.

Still, God invites us to reason with Him (v. 18). We reason within ourselves and among ourselves, but we do not want to accept God's reasoning. We want to be saved on our terms, not His.

When America is willing to turn from sin to God and accept His provision, willing and obedient, we shall eat the good of the land. If not, we shall be devoured with the sword, for "the mouth of the Lord hath spoken it."

## MAY 23

### LIVING BUT DEAD

*I know thy works, that thou hast a name that thou livest, and art dead.* REVELATION 3:1.

THE PRODIGAL WAS dead but came alive (Lk. 15:24). So it is with all who believe (Rom. 6:13). The Sardis church was alive but dead. It had a name to live, but Jesus had another name for it. The name we have for ourselves is not always what our Lord calls us. You say you have eternal life. Does God say so? Not every one who calls Him Lord, Lord, is known of Him. Some Christians seem active enough, but it is not the vitality of the spirit, it is only the vivacity of religious flesh. And how many busy churches are called live churches, while the Lord looks on and says, "Thou art dead." Does Jesus say that yours is a live church?

111

How does it look to Him? Mere activity does not deceive Him.

"She that liveth in pleasure is dead while she liveth." She may be animated and really get around, but God says "dead." And a lot of go-getter Christians and churches draw no better word from Him who looks on the heart.

Are you one who was once dead and now lives, or do you seem to live but are dead?

## MAY 24

### FRIENDS OF GOD

*And he was called the friend of God.* JAMES 2:23.

OF ALL THE preachers and teachers and religious folk of our day, how few impress us that they know God! Able and successful, earnest and aggressive, we find in them much that is good. But can we not count on our fingers those who have gone far into the deeper things of the Spirit, who have learned those precious secrets of intimacy with God? To how few could we go in an hour of deepest trouble, to how few dare we tell our inmost problems!

This age of phenobarbital and psychoses does not lend itself to a closer walk with God. The price is great nowadays, and he who chooses to be God's friend may be overlooked in the worship of celebrities. But in our better and needier moments we turn from heroes to seek some lowly soul who has learned those rare lessons of the school of Enoch who walked with God. Our efficient American Christianity is too busy putting things over to be interested in the quiet, slow saints who take time to be holy instead of just singing about it.

Give us more friends of God!

112

## MAY 25

### "AN HOLY MAN OF GOD"

*I perceive that this is an holy man of God.* II KINGS
4:9.

HOW MANY OF us modern prophets, do you suppose, ever
convey such an impression to the Shunammites of today?
The words "holy" and "holiness" have been joked about,
and to not a few a holy man means a queer fanatic with
long hair, robe, and sandals. But we are in dire need of
some "holy men of God" who may be out of style with
earth but are in step with heaven. The modern variety of
religious go-getter may dazzle us with brilliance and efficiency, but he does not make us think first either of holiness or God.

Said McCheyne: "Men return again and again to the
few who have mastered the spiritual secret, whose life has
been hid with Christ in God. These are of the old-time religion, hung to the nails of the cross."

We are weary of the success and happiness school. We
need holy men of God who are in touch with Headquarters,
who remind us of another world than this.

## MAY 26

### LAST GOD TO GO

*Lovers of their own selves.* II TIMOTHY 3:2.

SELF-LOVE TAKES many forms. Not only pride and vanity
and worldly ambition, but a sickly preoccupation with
one's own troubles, physical or otherwise. Such self-cen-
tered, ingrown souls make themselves the center of their
universe. Self thrives on attention. It grows as it is petted
and coddled, until it becomes a colossus dominating one's

113

lives and all others it can by making friends and loved ones the slaves of such self-worshipers.

The best treatment is neglect by becoming preoccupied with something or someone else. Such ailments disappear when ignored. The supreme preoccupation is not a mere person or cause but Christ Himself. That is why He asked us to deny self, take up the cross, and follow Him. That is why He bade us lose our lives to find them. When he fills our minds and hearts and lives other gods vanish. And no god is harder to topple from its shrine than self. It will gladly give up all lesser idols if only it be allowed to retain the throne.

## MAY 27

### REFUGE

*For ye are dead, and your life is hid with Christ in God.*
COLOSSIANS 3:3.

SOME ESCAPE THE tyranny of self to a great degree by a new vocation, a new love. But some day the vocation may have to be abandoned, the loved one may die. Christ offers us the highest deliverance, not in a cause or in a philosophy or even in "Christian work," but in Himself. Some dear souls become interested in a new truth like the victorious life and make a fad of it, but still do not get through to Him who is our life.

We are dead, our old self has been nailed to the cross and we are to reckon it a fact, yield ourselves to God and obey Him. It is the message of this third chapter of Colossians as of the sixth chapter of Romans. Self does not crucify self but submits to crucifixion as the Spirit works it out in experience. But we do not major on dying, we rise from the grave to walk in newness of life, freed from the shackles of the old life.

114

If we lose ourselves in anything less than Christ Himself there is no full deliverance. Only "with Christ in God" are we in a safe hiding place.

### STRATEGY FOR VICTORY

*Be not overcome of evil, but overcome evil with good.*
ROMANS 12:21.

"OVERCOME EVIL WITH good"—here is a principle often overlooked. We do not master our sins and doubts and fears by direct frontal assault, taking them one by one. It is better to concentrate on the positive, become occupied with the Lord, and leave these evils to die from neglect. General MacArthur did not take each Japanese outpost on the way back to the Philippines. He concentrated on a few major objectives and left the other enemy garrisons to "rot on the vine." If we become taken up with every temptation and difficulty we shall wear ourselves out on secondary skirmishes. Let us rather put on the Lord Jesus Christ and make not provision for the flesh. We can circumvent a lot of our worries by giving our attention to the good. Most of our ailments will die from neglect. We give them importance when we devote time and thought to them.

Make your life a major drive with Christ the objective—"This one thing I do"—and let the devil's minor outposts starve to death.

## MAY 29

### ABIDING AND OBEYING

*If ye keep my commandments, ye shall abide in my love.* JOHN 15:10.

THIS IS ONLY one of many verses that connect fellowship with Christ with obedience to Him. We are His friends if we do His commandments. If we do God's will we are Jesus' brother and sister. He that has and keeps His commandments, he it is that loves the Lord.

We are prone to make much of abiding, not much of obeying. We bask in the blessedness of being His friends, dwelling in Him, being hid with Christ in God. But Jesus always joins this holy estate with practical obedience. We hang up promises as mottoes but we are not so fond of commandments. Contemplation and adoration and mysticism have their place, but the friend of Jesus is the man who does what Christ commands him. To be sure, His commandment is that we love one another, but that includes a lot of other commandments and is as practical as the Thirteenth Chapter of First Corinthians.

A lot of people sing, "Oh, How I Love Jesus," who are not keeping His commandments. And He said, "If a man love me, he will keep my words."

## MAY 30

### PURPOSEFUL PRUNING

*Every branch that beareth fruit, he purgeth it, that it may bring forth more fruit.* JOHN 15:2.

"WHOM THE LORD loveth he chasteneth." The beloved child is chastised and the fruitful branch is pruned. Many a troubled soul in an hour of distress has fancied itself the object of God's displeasure. But it is the *fruitful* branch that feels the knife. The unfruitful branch is taken away and burned. Many a saint in adversity has feared that he is perhaps a stranger to grace, forgetting that it is the bastards, not sons, who escape the Father's discipline.

There is a purpose in the pruning, "that it may bring forth more fruit." Not the feverish stepped-up production of this machine age but the natural, spontaneous fruitfulness of the branch that draws its life from the vine. Too

116

much of our religious productivity is ground out by the methods of this age. The true Christian abides and abounds, and to him the Father-Husbandman's pruning is part of the process.

### NEARING HOME

*The time of my departure is at hand.* II TIMOTHY 4:6.

How OFTEN HAVE I noticed when headed home from my travels a relief and release, a lessening of strain and tension. Nothing bothers me, I feel great, I am going home!

Should it not be so with us Christian pilgrims who seek a country? Why should earth's cares pester us? We are on our way home, and nothing can stop us. Death itself but speeds the arrival and is a paying proposition, for "to depart and be with Christ is far better." "To die is gain."

"One sweetly solemn thought" daily reminds us that we are nearer home than we've ever been before. Let time and earth do their worst, they but quicken our heavenward pace! There is nothing to fear. No combination of men or devils can keep us from getting home. Why should I not be hilarious with a song in my heart? I shall soon be beyond all that spoils my peace and joy. My Lord is over there, and more and more of those I love gather on that side. Nothing can hinder me from arriving. I feel like traveling on!

It is great to be nearing home!

### JUNE 1

### DON'T STAY AT SHILOH!

*So the woman went her way, and did eat, and her countenance was no more sad.* I SAMUEL 1:18.

HANNAH HAD NOT been eating and she had been sad (v. 7). But now she had poured out her heart to God, and had entered into a covenant with Him, and she trusted Him for the answer to her prayer. Notice that she did not run up to Shiloh every day and "agonize" and pray the same prayer over and over. It would have looked very religious, but it would have been rankest unbelief. Instead she "went her way, and did eat," and resumed a normal life, "and her countenance was no more sad." She did not live in alternate hope and fear, she lived happily with a glad face. Some of us need sorely to learn a lesson from Hannah. It is no mark of piety to return to Shiloh every day fasting and weeping. Faith settles with God and then eats a good dinner and goes its way looking happy, not hoping but believing. Nervous, uncertain souls, forever begging God, are really unbelievers. Faith takes His Word for it and lives normally and happily.

Don't stay at Shiloh! Go your way, eat, and smile!


## JUNE 2

### HOLY DISGUST

*Therefore I will look unto the Lord; I will wait for the God of my salvation: my God will hear me.* MICAH 7:7.

"THEREFORE" LOOKS BACK to Micah's complaint, found in the preceding verses. It was an evil time. Micah found no good man about him. Men in authority worked in collusion to do evil. No confidence could be put in people, even in one's family. It reads like the morning newspaper!

But Micah was not left without an alternative. He looked unto the Lord. It is a fine thing when a man in high and holy disgust and distrust of the world around him turns to the world above him. Tired of all else, he thirsts for the living God in a dry and thirsty land where no water is.

Change and decay in all around I see;
O, Thou who changest not, abide with me!

118

When we grow sick of earth and all it has to offer, we are in good shape to look up. And as some saint has said, "We must get into us more of that which is above us or we shall give way to that which is around us."

### "PRAY THROUGH" AND "ONLY BELIEVE'"

*And as he passed over Penuel, the sun rose upon him, and he halted upon his thigh.* GENESIS 32:31.

THE "PRAY IT THROUGH" and "Take It By Faith" schools have argued through the centuries and many a soul has been confused thereby. Some have "sought" and "tarried" and exhausted themselves agonizing to no avail. Others have mistaken laziness for passivity and have made a feigned faith an excuse for not resolutely pressing through to God. There is truth in both schools: one must mean business and come to a point of crisis; but, still, all we get from God simple faith must take.

Jacob did not win by wrestling. God crippled him and he ended by clinging. Sunrise at Penuel found him limping, but he had power with God and men. Paul did not pray through until his thorn was removed, but he learned to take by faith grace sufficient for each day. Jacob meant business and so did Paul. But beyond that they walked by simple faith and obedience. It may take wrestling to reach the point of abandonment. After that we cling in humble dependence.

### END AND BEGINNING

*Woe is me! for I am undone.* ISAIAH 6:5.

ISAIAH HAS COME to the end of himself. Like Moses in Midian, like Job when he saw God, like Daniel with his comeliness turned to corruption and Habakkuk with rottenness entering his bones; like Peter at Tiberias and Paul with his thorn, he has come to the end of all feeling and trying and praying, the end of all he is and has, to where God begins.

Blessed is that hour of holy desperation when a man reaches that extremity which is God's opportunity and moves out of the wreck of himself into Christ. Nothing in his hand he brings, but just as he is without one plea he takes up residence with Christ in God. He puts no value on anything he has or is, attaches no importance to his feelings or faith or prayers. Christ is everything. We waste many years trying to construct some sort of refuge out of the rubbish of ourselves, until we abandon it all and dwell in Another. From then on we have no confidence in the flesh but humbly look unto Him for salvation and the "all things" that go with it, His sufficient grace for the whole man, for every day, for any need, that we, having all sufficiency in all things, may abound to every good work.

## JUNE 5

### BELIEVING IS OBEYING

*And this is his commandment, That we should believe on the name of his Son Jesus Christ, and love one another, as he gave us commandment.* I JOHN 3:23.

IT IS OFTEN overlooked that God *commands* us to believe. He does not merely invite or urge, He commands it. Living in unbelief or uncertainty is outright disobedience. We do not honor God by indecision and doubt. It is faith that pleases Him. We ought to come to Christ immediately and trust Him and never waver, because He has bidden us come and believe and we can do anything we ought to do. He inclines us to come by His Spirit, for certainly neither the flesh nor the devil ever impelled a man toward Christ.

You may be sure that He is working in you to will and do of His good pleasure, and if you will to obey Him by believing as best you know how, you may be certain He will not cast you out.

It is simple obedience to believe. Therefore "repent ye and believe the gospel." "God commandeth all men everywhere to repent." "And this is his commandment, that we should believe."

## JUNE 6

### "TRYING TO REST"

*Let us labor therefore to enter into that rest.* HEBREWS 4:11.

WE DO NOT labor to rest. That is a contradiction. We labor to enter into rest, we make it our resolute purpose, we go about it in dead earnest. But when we have ceased from our works and entered, then we rest. We make an effort to reach a vacation spot but after we arrive we rest. The Saviour invites us to His rest, and we are not to live in a tense strain, holding on to it for dear life for fear "it" will slip from us. We do not keep Him, He keeps us. We are His guest, not His host, we sit at His table and we need never go away.

The rest of the Christian is not a pose of faith rigidly fixed and maintained. It is not something we screw ourselves up to, it is the very opposite of all strenuous effort. We labor to enter in, we earnestly commit all in a positive, definite, businesslike way. Then the responsibility is His to keep what we have committed; we have simply to abide. Like some vacationists, we exhaust ourselves trying to rest! Let go and let God!

121

## JUNE 7

### STEPPING IN THE LIGHT

*As ye have therefore received Christ Jesus the Lord,
so walk ye in him.* COLOSSIANS 2:6.

GOD WOULD NOT have us merely "take a stand," He would
have us walk. Too many have taken a stand and are still
standing; for years they have made no progress. The New
Testament makes much of our walk. We walk by faith, not
by sight. We are to walk in the light, walk in love, walk in
newness of life, walk worthy of our vocation, walk circumspectly, walk worthy of the Lord, walk honestly, walk in
the truth, walk as He walked. The Christian life begins with
a step of faith—"As ye have therefore received Christ Jesus
the Lord"—and it proceeds step by step—"so walk ye in
him."

We are inclined to take a stand and at best strive to
maintain it instead of walking daily with God like Enoch.
Faith grows as we go. And don't let your tongue get too far
ahead of your feet. Let your walk match your talk!


## JUNE 8

### ITCHING EARS AND BURNING HEARTS

*For the time will come when they will not endure
sound doctrine; but after their own lusts shall they
heap to themselves teachers, having itching ears.* II
TIMOTHY 4:3.
*Did not our hearts burn within us while he talked with
us by the way and while he opened to us the scriptures?* LUKE 24:32.

IT IS A day of itching ears. Men chase popular preachers
who can entertain. Religion is just another fad. And not a
few Christians who pass as lovers of sound doctrine can-

not endure its application, but move from preacher to preacher, church to church, listening to their pet Paul or Apollos or Cephas. A lot of what goes for Bible teaching and evangelism is but religious entertainment. Men are not moved within to the point of obedience. They have itching ears.

We need an outbreak of holy heartburn, when hearers shall be doers, when congregations shall go out from meetings to do things for God and men instead of pleasantly gossiping while the fowls of the air snatch up the seed of the Word.

God move us from itching-ear retreats to burning-heart revivals!

## JUNE 9

### LOOK OUT FOR THE DEVIL!

*Be sober, be vigilant; because your adversary the devil, as a roaring lion, walketh about, seeking whom he may devour.* I PETER 5:8.

WE NEED NOT be surprised if, right on the heels of a new spiritual beginning, we are beset with double force by the devil. It is a good sign. It is evidence that we are making progress and have aroused him. He will attack body, mind, and spirit to disable, deceive, or discourage. He will make us dull and stupid, will deaden our spirits and lull us into a stupor. A sense of things present will come doubly strong and heaven will seem far away. Unexplainable things will happen and we may feel that God has forsaken us. Right when we expected ecstasy we shall meet melancholy. Instead of raptures, we shall encounter boredom and wonder why we feel more like sighing than shouting.

Be not discouraged. It is a sure sign of progress. The farther you go, the more you may meet with. But greater is He who is in you than he who is in the world. Your Ally has conquered your Adversary.

## "THE WALL"

*For thou hast been a strength to the poor, a strength to the needy in his distress, a refuge from the storm, a shadow from the heat, when the blast of the terrible ones is as a storm against the wall.* ISAIAH 25:4.

How OFTEN IN the loneliness and strain of our work, when foes, seen and unseen, beset us, we have been conscious of an invisible wall, the angel of the Lord encamping round about us to deliver us. Often we have been helpless, with no strength of our own against the enemy. Yet we have been able to lie down and sleep, conscious that our Keeper never slumbers. "The wall" is a good figure, for we need not be roofed in overhead. Satan can surround us but he cannot roof us over, and we need the upward look unobstructed. Never has God's wall broken down, nor has the Adversary breached it. Because it is invisible, the devil would have us fear it is not there; but it is. He can come so far but no farther.

If ever we needed a wall, it is now. The hosts of evil are making their worst mad assaults, and no ramparts of our own can avail. But we have a fortress, a hiding place, a Rock of Ages. Are you hid with Christ in God?

## "COME BEFORE WINTER

*Do thy diligence to come before winter.* II TIMOTHY 4:21.

"IT IS NOT good that the man should be alone." Adam had God in the Garden of Eden, but he still needed Eve, and

God knew it. We must have human companionship. Paul had no wife, so he turned to his friends, and to Timothy, his "beloved son" in particular. He urged first, "Do thy diligence to come shortly unto me" (v. 9); then he thought of approaching cold weather and of what it would add to his loneliness, so he repeats his request and says, "Come before winter." It is a touching sidelight on a great soul, but human like us all.

Winter has a way of coming in varied forms, and blessed is the fellowship of a kindred soul. We have the Lord, but He Himself has recognized that we need the touch of a human hand. He Himself came down and lived among us as a man. We cannot see Him now, but blest be the tie that binds human hearts in Christian love. Most precious of earthly ties is husband and wife "in the Lord." If Paul is denied a wife he had better find a Timothy. And may Timothy arrive before winter!

## JUNE 12

### GOD'S STIMULANT

*And be not drunk with wine, wherein is excess; but be filled with the Spirit.* EPHESIANS 5:18.

How THIS POOR world seeks release and escape through drink but instead of happiness reaps a headache! God has provided a stimulant for His people in the power of the Holy Spirit. And there is no wretched "morning after" with a dark brown taste! "The blessing of the Lord, it maketh rich, and he addeth no sorrow with it" (Prov. 10:22). The early Christians were accused of being full of new wine. They had the wine of heaven, of which all the wines of earth are but poor imitations.

125

And, mind you, the thought here is that of a stimulant, not a sedative. Unless something stirs us we are worthless. All the world's excitements fail to afford a proper stimulus. And a lot of our modern religious "rousements" are but substitutes for the wine of the Spirit, often the old Adam whooping it up in church.

Every other wine runs easily to excess. Only the Christian filled with the Spirit has an adequate stimulant to carry him through these days.

## JUNE 13

### ANTIDOTE TO SELF-PITY

*Most gladly therefore will I rather glory in my infirmities, that the power of Christ may rest upon me.*
II CORINTHIANS 12:9.

AFTER PAUL EMERGES from his height-to-depth experience of the third heaven and thorn in the flesh to rest in the sufficient grace of Christ, he takes pleasure in infirmities, reproaches, necessities, persecutions, distresses for Christ's sake, for when he is weak then he is strong. He rejoices in the very weakness that drives him to Christ. He does not grumble, he glories. And he does not go on a spree of self-pity. What an opportunity to feel sorry for himself with this trouble that God would not take away!

If God grants you neither a third-heaven experience nor the removal of your thorn, rejoice in whatever He uses to bring you to simple daily dependence on Christ. But do not merely glory in infirmities. Finish the sentence . . . "that the power of Christ may rest upon me." All else is incidental to that. Let us major on His strength, not on our weakness.

126

## JUNE 14

### WEATHER WATCHERS

*He that observeth the wind shall not sow; and he that regardeth the clouds shall not reap.* ECCLESIASTES 11:4.

IF A FARMER waited until he was sure of the weather he would never raise a crop. He has to reckon with the weather and contend with it, but he cannot be sure of it. So every year he makes a venture of faith.

We cannot let the wind and clouds of circumstance determine our course. We cannot grow a harvest for God with one eye on the weather. Just as with the farmer, circumstances are to be considered, and we shall not foolishly disregard them. But we must not let them be the main factor in making our decisions.

Too many saints live fearfully from one "weather report" to another, scanning the skies and watching the clouds, conscious of "conditions" rather than of Christ. Faith goes ahead in fair weather and foul. It breaks up the fallow ground, sows the seed, cultivates the crop, and gathers the harvest. There may be pests and floods and droughts, but the Lord of the Harvest will see to it that our labor is not in vain.

## JUNE 15

### A BETTER WAY

*Jesus could no more openly enter into the city, but was without in desert places: and they came to him from every quarter.* MARK 1:45.

LET THE BIBLE scholars account for it as they will, over and over again Jesus discouraged publicity, left the crowd

127

for the solitudes, and never played up to the multitude. His brethren could not understand why He did not go up to Jerusalem and get in the public eye. He did not seek the crowd, the crowd sought Him.

All this would be quite incomprehensible to this age of ballyhoo and the despair of high-pressure advertising. The Early Church grew as one brought another, and the Lord added such as should be saved. The Gospel was its own best publicity. By word of mouth it was noised about. Today we build up a gigantic publicity after the fashion of this age, but what we advertise does not come up to the advance notices. The mountain brings forth a mouse.

God's ways are not ours and the church did her mightiest work unassisted by radio, television, and modern advertising. The best publicity the Gospel will ever have is a new Christian out to win others. And simple arithmetic shows that if each new disciple brought another the statistics would soon be phenomenal.

Maybe we have it all figured out wrong. Think it over.

## JUNE 16

### ABHORRENCE, NOT TOLERANCE

*Abhor that which is evil; cleave to that which is good.*
ROMANS 12:9.

WE ARE NOT to tolerate evil but abhor it. The mood of the age is to put up with evil, allow it, and then move easily to play with it and finally practice it. Tolerance is a pet word these days, and we stretch our consciences while we "broaden" our minds. But the Word of God tells us that the fear of the Lord is to hate evil and that we are to abstain from the very appearance of evil. There is no leniency toward sin whatever in that. Nothing is more dangerous to our spiritual well-being than a mild amiability that smiles at sin. Some have come to think that there is something noble in a mild attitude toward sin. Compassion on the sinful is one thing, but never confuse it with tolerance of evil. We have sunk to an acceptance of that toward which God counsels abhorrence and behold the harvest!

A holy, healthy hatred of sin and indignation at evil is our crying need today, because we fear not God—and the fear of the Lord is to hate evil.

## JUNE 17

### "WATERS THAT GO SOFTLY"

*Forasmuch as this people refuseth the waters of Shiloah that go softly . . . the Lord bringeth up upon them the waters of the river, strong and many.* Isaiah 8:6, 7.

THREATENED BY INVASION from Israel and Syria, Ahaz of Judah foolishly chose alliance with Assyria instead of reliance on God. The soft-flowing waters of Shiloah represent the benign reign of the house of David as compared with the violent Euphrates, emblem of the Assyrians.

How prone we are to choose earthly alliances, confederacies of the world and the flesh, instead of God's gentle way! The way of the meek and lowly, the rule of love, seems too weak to cope with the ways and devices of men. The world chooses the way of the Euphrates and suffers a deluge of disaster. And in our private lives the still small voice and the quiet way of God seem too mild for some of us. We ally with the boisterous, turbulent spirit of the age and live to regret it. For Assyria always comes to help but remains to conquer.

Remember, it is the *Lamb* that finally conquers!

129

## CARMEL AND HOREB

*Then the fire of the Lord fell . . .* I Kings 18:38.
*But the Lord was not in the fire: and after the fire a still,*
*small voice.* I Kings 19:12.

God was in the fire at Carmel; He was not in the fire at Horeb. We are not to gather from the still, small voice that God is never in wind, earthquake, and fire. He often is. He came at Pentecost with a sound as of a rushing mighty wind. He came in an earthquake in the Philippian jail.

God works in nature in the cataclysmic, in flood and tornado; and He works in the gradual, quiet process of the seasons. He works in mighty mass movements in revival with a Whitefield or a Moody. But He also moves in quiet gatherings in the day-by-day work of faith and labor of love among the churches.

And into our hearts He sometimes breaks in sudden and tempestuous ways, in mountain-top raptures and third-heaven experiences. But He also works in daily growth in the knowledge of Christ, the quiet walk by His sufficient grace.

You cannot live at Carmel all the time. Carmel happens only once in a while. God is at Horeb too—if you have ears to hear.

## JUNE 19

### PROPHETIC AND PASTORAL

*And he gave some, . . . prophets; and some evangelists;*
*and some, pastors and teachers.* Ephesians 4:11.

In the middle ages the church retired into solitude and seclusion and God had to raise up awakeners. There come high tides of revival and evangelism, and God balances them with pastors and teachers. Moody was a messenger to the multitudes, but he had the good judgment to associate with him men like Morgan and Meyer, who could teach and build up the saints.

We must have both. If we have only teachers we may become passive Bible students and fail of aggressive evangelism. We may spend ourselves in public activity and starve the inner life. The church needs both and the individual Christian needs both. It is pitiable indeed if the evangelist disparages the work of the teacher or the teacher belittles mass evangelism.

Some saints need a prophet to blast them out of a comfortable quietism. Some need a teacher to make them be still and take in that they may have something to give out.

Our Lord combined both in His perfect ministry, quietly teaching His disciples and shepherding His flock, while at the same time He was a prophet and challenged us to a life of service in His Name.

## JUNE 20

### ARE YOU GOD'S ENEMY?

*Whosoever therefore will be a friend of the world is the enemy of God.* JAMES 4:4.
*If any man love the world, the love of the Father is not in him.* I JOHN 2:15.

How CONCLUSIVE THESE statements! The friend of the world makes himself thereby the enemy of God. We would not use so strong a term as "enemy," but God does. "The friendship of this world is enmity with God." Not mild disagreement but utter hostility!

And John does not say that if any man love the world the love of the Father is weak in him—it is not in him at all. Why is it that we hear so little of this today? Because Christians and churches that have compromised with the world

131

and gone into alliance with it are in no position to say "amen" to such an unequivocal pronouncement as this. We have become artists at soft-pedaling Bible verses that come too uncomfortably close to where we live, and these certainly are two that are played pianissimo while we pull out all the stops on others.

But no exegetical sleight of hand can tone down these texts. The friend of the world is God's enemy. The lover of the world has no love of God in him.

## JUNE 21

### HOLY QUIETNESS

*Study to be quiet.* I THESSALONIANS 4:11.

ONE OF OUR national leaders some years ago expressed doubt as to whether there could have been a Constitution of the United States if the Convention had been currently reported by radio, telegraph, and newspapers over the thirteen colonies. Now, with television added, he might wonder some more. The tempo of the times and our publicity gadgets have had a devastating effect on contemplation and deliberation. It shows up in the documents and dissertations we are turning out.

Unless somebody gets still long enough to hear from God we are going to have scant word from heaven these days. Our Lord made the people sit down before He fed them. Samuel said to Saul, "Stand thou still a while, that I may shew thee the word of God." We are all living in a commotion and we do not know how to break out of the frenzy. Solitude is maddening to us, for we run in herds.

Habakkuk was in a stew of complaint about the times until he got off to his tower to hear what God would say. In our text Paul is calming some overexcited saints—and we could take a few lessons today!

132

## "BEHOLD YOUR SAVIOR COME!"

*Behold the Lamb of God which taketh away the sin of the world.* JOHN 1:29.

WE OFTEN HEAR these days the question, "What is the world coming to?" It is an interesting subject and most of the discussion relieves the speakers but not the situation. The chief theme of the Gospel is not what the world is coming to but rather the One who has come to the world.

It is also very popular now to behold the sin of the world. There never was more of it and it never was more evident. But John the Baptist was pointing out the cure for sin, the Lamb who came to take it away.

Of course, there is a very real sense in which men need to see their sin and themselves to be sinners. There has not been enough preaching on sin with that in view. But the Gospel is Good News that the problem of our sin finds its answer in the person of God's Son. He has been made sin—not a sinner or sinful, but sin—for us, though He knew no sin, that we might be made the righteousness of God in Him.

Let us not be so taken up with beholding the sin of the world that we do not behold Him who came to take it away.

## CARNALITY WITH A HALO

*For ye are yet carnal: . . . are ye not carnal, and walk as men?* I CORINTHIANS 3:3.

LET IT BE observed that the marks of carnality Paul had in mind here were not card-playing, dancing, and theater-going. They are, indeed, marks of carnality, but Paul was concerned with some sins we overlook while we lambast other forms of evil. "Whereas there is among you envying, and strife, and divisions, are ye not carnal, and walk as men? For while one saith, I am of Paul; and another, I am of Apollos; are ye not carnal?"

Some who have long prided themselves that they do not smoke or haunt the movies seem not to have discovered that in their partyism and church strife they are just as carnal as the worldlings they censure.

Nothing has harmed the cause of Christ more than the Paul-Cephas-Apollos factions. And they are all the more deceptive because such carnality looks so much like zeal for the truth. "Nothing is so like conviction as simple obstinacy," and more than one dear brother has fancied himself Mr. Valiant-for-truth when, indeed, he is Mr. Fond-of-a-fight.

Be sure your "conviction" is not carnality.

## JUNE 24
### YOU CAN DO WHAT YOU OUGHT

*Lord, what wilt thou have me to do?* Acts 9:6.
*I can do all things through Christ which strengtheneth me.* Philippians 4:13.

Paul did not mean that he could do anything he wanted to do or some foolish thing. He could do all things that God wanted him to do.

We can do anything we ought to do, anything He wants us to do. And that leaves plenty of room for miracles! There is wide latitude within the limits of God's will. We shall not feel cramped.

There is much we know is God's will without making further inquiry. There is more of His will that opens up as we trust and obey. He would not ask us to do what cannot be done. But it is done through Christ, who keeps on pouring His power into us. His strength is made perfect in weakness, "that the power of Christ may rest upon us."

134

We can do all the work that is within His will. He who said, "Go ye," said, "Lo, I am with you," and "All power is given unto me."

## CALLED TO GO

*Whom shall I send, and who will go for us?* ISAIAH 6:8.

THERE ARE TWO sides to this stupendous proposition, His sending and our going. Some are called who do not go, like the son who promised to work in the vineyard but went not. Some go who are not sent: "I have not sent these prophets, yet they ran" (Jer. 23:21).

What a supreme privilege that the God of the Universe can use us in His business—"Whom shall I send?" Yet He never compels us nor violates our freedom of will—"Who will go for us?" His eyes run to and fro throughout the whole earth looking for someone who will go—not someone who will merely sing about it or say, "Here am I, send somebody else."

Never mind whether or not the mission will be a success. Isaiah was told that his hearers would not receive his message. We are not called to succeed, we are called to go.

And when we go He goes along!

## FIRM AND FRUITFUL

*Therefore, my beloved brethren, be ye stedfast, unmoveable, always abounding in the work of the Lord, forasmuch as ye know that your labor is not in vain in the Lord.* I CORINTHIANS 15:58.

WE HAVE HERE a good combination of firmness and fruitfulness. Some saints impress us with their fixity of belief, their sturdy orthodoxy, but they seem not to be abounding in God's work. They are like tombstones, not trees, by rivers of water. Paul gives us this double-barreled idea again: "Rooted and built up in him, and stablished in the faith, as ye have been taught, abounding therein with thanksgiving" (Col. 2:7). Rock-ribbed and radiant! Alas, the steadfast are not always singing and the singing are not always steadfast!

I suppose we shall always have the unmoveables who do not joyfully abound and the abounding who do not always abide, but blessed is the man who achieves by grace a good synthesis of both. Grounded and grateful! True and thankful! Stedfast and singing! Abiding and abounding! Theology and doxology!

## JUNE 27

### FEASTING AND SHARING

*Go your way, eat the fat, and drink the sweet, and send portions unto them for whom nothing is prepared.*
NEHEMIAH 8:10.

THE REVIVAL UNDER Ezra was built around the Word of God. The Gospel is neither a funeral nor a frolic but a feast and our duty is threefold. We are to "eat the fat," feed on the solid and substantial doctrine of the Book. We are also to "drink the sweet." The Word is not only strengthening but sweetening, sweeter than honey and the honeycomb. Some believers are strong but not sweet.

Then we are to send portions to them for whom nothing is prepared. We are to share, like Samson, with his hands full of honey fresh from his encounter with the lion.

So the Gospel feast means strength and sweetness and sharing. We do not fully experience what God has provided until we participate in all three. A true revival, like this one of Ezra's day, eats the fat and drinks the sweet and sends portions to them for whom nothing is prepared.

## "AN ENEMY HATH DONE THIS"

*Wherefore we would have come unto you, even I Paul, once and again; but Satan hindered us.* I THESSALONIANS 2:18.

STRANGE STATEMENT! WE are in the habit of saying, "I was providentially hindered." Not so Paul. He blames the devil. And remember that he called his thorn in the flesh "a messenger of Satan." He did not make God the author of it, though God did permit it. Did not our Lord say of the woman with a spirit of infirmity, "this woman whom Satan hath bound"? He told His disciples, "And Satan shall cast some of you into prison." We are too inclined to attribute to God the work of the devil, just as some have ascribed to the devil the work of God.

Paul gloried in tribulation, but we tend to glorify tribulation, which is something else. God does, indeed, permit Satan to afflict Job, but Job goes far afield if he thinks that sickness, pain, and death are of God. It sounds pious to look at the mischief and misery which Satan has wrought and call it providential. In the world we shall have tribulation, which we can turn to good account, but let us be intelligent and "give the devil his due."

### FINISHING GRACE

*Now also when I am old and greyheaded, O God, forsake me not; until I have shewed thy strength unto this generation, and thy power to every one that is to come.* PSALM 71:18.

THE PSALMIST PRAYS that he may demonstrate God in his old age, both to his own generation and to all who are to come, even as he has declared God in his youth. It is a worthy ambition. The eyes of the Lord are looking for someone in whose behalf He may show *Himself* strong, and the Psalmist wants to demonstrate God's strength, not his own. Paul lived to demonstrate Christ's strength made perfect in his weakness.

We are seeing a demon-stration of the powers of darkness these days. We need a demonstration of God in human lives. Too many of us are showing what we can do. The Psalmist wanted to show what God could do. He wanted to finish in old age what he had begun in youth. Some declare God in early life, deny Him in later years. Paul wanted to finish his course with joy.

Pray God for finishing grace!

## JUNE 30

### THANKS FOR VICTORY

*Thanks be to God, which giveth us the victory through our Lord Jesus Christ.* I CORINTHIANS 15:57.

OBSERVE THE *source* of our victory—"Thanks be unto God." The Blesser is greater than the blessing. Consider the *nature* of our victory—"which *giveth* us the victory." It is the gift of God. "Thanks be unto God for His unspeakable *gift*." And behold the *means* of our victory—"through *Jesus Christ our Lord*."

It is *total* victory over sin, death, and the grave. It is *daily* victory. Every heart ought to be a "victory garden." And it is *final* victory.

"This is the victory that overcometh the world, even our faith." It does not explain the world, nor endure it, nor enjoy it—it overcomes the world. But not just any kind of faith. It must be faith in our Lord Jesus Christ, for our victory is through Him.

Every day is V-Day when our faith is in Him. And every day is Thanksgiving Day for the victory through Him.

## JULY 1

### "HITHERTO . . ."

*Hitherto hath the Lord helped us.* I SAMUEL 7:12.

IT WAS ON this date one year ago that my wife faced serious surgery scheduled for next morning. We opened our daily devotional reading for that evening and found it headed "Eben-ezer . . . Hitherto hath the Lord helped us." We encouraged ourselves in the Lord our God as did David of old, confident that the same grace which had brought us safe "thus far" would be sufficient from there on. The God of the Hitherto is the God of the Henceforth!

The backward look is a good look if we review the path already trod to raise our Ebenezer and sing, "Hither by Thy help I'm come." This is the way to check with the past in order to cope with the future. The faithfulness of God will stand our inventory any time. We shall find that "there failed not ought of any good thing which the Lord had spoken . . . all came to pass."

And be sure to give God credit. Don't call it your wits or luck or fortune. Let your testimony be, "Hitherto hath *the Lord* helped us." Some have reversed Ebenezer to read, "Hitherto have I helped the Lord." "Tell how great things *the Lord* hath done for thee."

## JULY 2

### "HE WOULD HAVE PASSED BY"

*He cometh unto them, walking upon the sea,* and would have passed by them. MARK 6:48.

WITH THE EMMAUS disciples, "he made as though he would have gone further." Here He walks the waves, while the amazed disciples suppose they have seen a spirit. He assures them, "It is I."

Joseph and Mary supposed He was with them when He was not. Here others supposed He was not with them when He was. Mary in the garden supposed Him to be the gardener. No wonder the old Negro maid said, "I never sposes. Dem sposes will get you into trouble."

When the storm rages, He is there. But He will pass by if you do not avail yourself of His presence. "He would have passed by them. . . . He made as though he would have gone further." Call upon Him. "Pass me not, O gentle Saviour: do not pass me by."

He came to them in their distress, but He did not come into the boat until they called. He did not go into the Emmaus home until they constrained Him. He will not intrude. There is a point beyond which He will not go. If we do not invite Him in, He will go on.

<br>

### JULY 3

## ORIGIN AND OBJECT OF GOD'S CHASTISEMENT

*Whom the Lord loveth he chasteneth.* HEBREWS 12:6.

WHEN TROUBLE COMES our way we are apt to overlook this blessed fact. If we had no chastening we might well inquire whether we are children of God. This passage (5:11) is very explicit: if we are without chastisement we are bastards, not sons. Of course, the ungodly have plenty of trouble, and the way of the transgressor is hard, but the affliction of the unrighteous is not the chastisement of the Father. They are not His sons.

In this day of light and loose and lunatic notions of child-rearing, of course discipline does not mean much. But God has not been converted to the new pattern. Verse 9 says, "We have had fathers of our flesh which corrected us and we gave them reverence." Alas, too many fathers have not corrected, and too many children have no reverence for

140

fathers or for God. But the obedient Christian accepts God's discipline, seeks to learn its lessons, and gains the peaceable fruit of righteousness. God's purpose is that we might be partakers of His holiness. Surely that is worth all it costs.

But never forget this: God's chastening originates in His love. Because we are partakers of the Divine nature, His children, He disciplines us in order that we might be partakers of His holiness.

## JULY 4

### "WHEREFORE" AND "THEREFORE"

*Wherefore Jesus . . . suffered without the gate. Let us go forth therefore unto him without the camp.* HE-BREWS 13:12, 13.

JESUS KEPT HIS "wherefore" and I must keep my "therefore." He went without the gate to suffer and I must go outside the camp to serve. I am not merely to go *from* something, I am to go *to* Him. Where He is I belong. And it is not His popularity but His reproach that I must bear. The world and some churches have devised a popular Christ, but He is not this Christ of the Wherefore. One can stay inside the camp and follow this fictitious Jesus, but not the One who suffered that I might be sanctified with His blood. This present age, like all ages past, despises a bleeding Christ and a gory cross. There is nothing elegant about following a crucified Saviour and seeking a city to come.

I cannot get by with singing about the wondrous cross. Love so amazing, so divine, demands my soul, my life, my all. His "wherefore" demands my "therefore." And that means the sacrifice of person: "Let *us* . . . (v. 13), of praise (v. 15), of possessions (v. 16)

"Jesus paid it all" in the Wherefore. "All to Him I owe" in the Therefore.

141

## JULY 5

### FAITH OR "IT"?

*According to your faith be it unto you.* MATTHEW 9:29.

"ACCORDING TO YOUR faith be *it* . . ." Be what? How much does "it" include? Here is one of the smallest and one of the biggest words—small in the dictionary but large in our text! For "it" includes all our need which God will supply according to His riches in glory by Christ Jesus. And the measure of that supply is "according to your faith." You may have all you need and all that faith will take. Whether that need be trivial or tremendous makes no difference to God—everything is His, anyway. You need not mind bringing to Him the simplest matter. The sparrow's fall does not escape His notice. Nor will you strain the heavenly resources with a stupendous request. The ocean will hold up a boat or a battleship, and God's grace will stand any weight you put on it.

So, whatever "it" may be that you are facing, no matter how hard or hopeless "it" may seem, do not let "it" dominate your faith, make "it" submit to your faith. "According to your faith be *it*" is God's yardstick, not "According to *it* be your faith."

Are you living by the tyranny of "it" or by the Triumph of Faith?

### JULY 6

### "AND TODAY"

*Jesus Christ the same yesterday,* and today, *and forever.* HEBREWS 13:8.

IT IS SAID that George Muller kept on his desk a motto bearing the central words of our text, "AND TODAY.' Well might he do so and surely few men have demonstrated better the truth of it. It is not difficult to believe in Jesus Christ the same yesterday. And He will prove one day that He is the same forever. But "Jesus Christ the same *today*" —what a time we have with that middle span! Amid the dull monotony of things as they are, when the skies seem leaden and nothing breaks on the uninteresting scene, it is easier to visualize the Christ of the Galilean Past or the Christ of the Glorious Future than to expect great things from the Christ of the Glamourless Now.

But our text stoutly insists *and today*. We may not see Him in the flesh as they saw Him yesterday, and we see not yet all things put under Him as one day we shall, but He said He would be with us "all the days," and that includes today.

Is not many a Christian experience like this verse with "and today" in very fine type—strong in faith in the Christ of yesterday and forever, but very weak in faith in His presence and power today?

## JULY 7

### WHY TROUBLE THE MASTER?

*Thy daughter is dead: why troublest thou the Master any further?* MARK 5:35.

"THE LITTLE GIRL is dead. It is too late now. Why bother the Master and take up His time?"

Have you come to a place where the case seems hopeless, where the prospect is "dead"? That loved one for whom you have prayed so long seems in direr straits than ever. The hope long deferred now seems impossible.

But Jesus had no funerals. And when the world says the issue is as dead as a corpse, remember that Jesus can break up funerals. We are so prone to give up and attend the interment of our hopes when God would raise the dead.

Jesus said to the ruler, "Be not afraid, only believe." And so He says to you. When ordinary logic, when undiscerning friends say, "It is too late," be not afraid to "trouble the Master."

Only believe . . . .
All things are possible,
Only believe!


## JULY 8

### SAD OR GLAD?

*For they all saw him, and were troubled.* MARK 6:50.
*Then were the disciples glad, when they saw the Lord.*
JOHN 20:20.

THE DISCIPLES SAW Him in a storm but supposed Him to be a spirit. They did not recognize Him. But in our second verse they saw the risen Lord and knew Him by the print of the nails in His hands and feet.

Surely the sight of the Lord should make us glad. But sometimes we wist not that it is He. He draws near, but, like the Emmaus disciples, we have holden eyes. What should thrill us only troubles us. Indeed, as the Emmaus disciples related their experience, Jesus appeared, but they "supposed that they had seen a spirit." He quelled their fears then as He did in John's account by showing the marks of the cross.

We walk by faith, not by sight, these days, and are not granted a view of Him with our eyes. But in His dealings with us He still walks our seas and comes into our rooms through doors we have shut. Alas, that fear so often sees a spirit when faith should see the Saviour! What should bring triumph then brings only trouble. See Him and be glad!

144

## HURT BEFORE HEALING

*Wherefore come out from among them, and be ye separate, saith the Lord, and touch not the unclean thing: and I will receive you, and will be a Father unto you, and ye shall be my sons and daughters, saith the Lord Almighty.* II CORINTHIANS 6:17, 18.

THERE CAN BE no normal Father-and-son fellowship until sin has been dealt with and put away. It is all very well to talk of just leading a normal daily Christian life without having to be "revived," but most Christians are not ready to lead such a life. One might as well tell a sick man to get out in the sunshine and follow his usual habits. We are subnormal and abnormal, and sometimes drastic measures are necessary before we can be normal Christians again. Even surgery may be indicated and the offending eye or foot or hand must be removed. We let Christians and churches go on in their sick condition rather than remove infection and employ spiritual catharsis. Sometimes radical procedure is necessary, and it may be disturbing to sick souls who prefer to be unmolested, but there can be no recovery without it.

Paul followed this course with the Corinthians, and our Lord called for repentance among the ailing churches of Asia. Sometimes we must feel worse before we can feel better. Hurt often must come before healing.

## JULY 10

### WHEN THE BEST FRIEND FAILS

*Mine own familiar friend, in whom I trusted, which did eat of my bread, hath lifted up his heel against me. But thou, O Lord . . .* PSALM 41:9, 10.

WE MIGHT AS well face it: most of us meet some sad disillusionments and heartaches at the hands of our friends.

The servant of God will learn that while God never fails him, God's people sometimes do. He will learn to expect little of people but much of God. We must make up our minds—"Am I going to trust God or not?" People will fail me, my very best friend may forsake me, but God will make up any deficits in His own way. Either we carry on with a childlike trust or we become sour and suspicious and hard-boiled, we worry and scheme by our own wits to "give as good as we get," and that does disastrous things to us as Christians. Of course, we are not to be gullible simpletons, but it is better to be wronged once in a while by people we trusted than to grow cynical after the pattern of this world. When it is all over, we shall find that God evened it up and took care of us, even though some of His people failed. We are winners after all if we stay sweet, though we may be losers at the hands of men.

## JULY 11

### "AND FORSAKETH"

*He that covereth his sins shall not prosper: but whoso confesseth and forsaketh them shall have mercy.* PROVERBS 28:13.

"IF WE CONFESS our sins"—sins of omission, the things we should do but are not doing; sins of commission, the things we should not do but are doing; sins of disposition, sins of the spirit, so often overlooked in our emphasis on sins of the body; and doubtful things. "Whatsoever is not of faith is sin."

Confession should be accompanied by renunciation—"and forsaketh them." "If my people shall . . . turn from their wicked ways." Someone has said, "We cannot expect God to take away our sins by forgiving them if we will not put them away by forsaking them." All too often there is a cheap and easy confession of sin: "We have done many things we should not have done, and have left undone many things which we should have done." Who hasn't? Such confession does not forsake sin and turn from wicked ways.

Have you made a clean break with your sins and burned the bridges behind you?


## JULY 12

### ETERNAL TRUTH, PRESENT FACT

*Faith is the substance of things hoped for, the evidence of things not seen.* HEBREWS 11:1.

FAITH SOMETIMES MEANS a calm, quiet, passive, humble confidence that goes on its way, resting not in itself but in the Faithful One. But there is the other aspect, when faith becomes "an affirmation and an act that bids eternal truth be present fact." There is a reckless, almost fierce, faith that laughs in the teeth of circumstance and shouts, like Paul in the storm, "I believe God," and affirms, though a legion of demons mock, "Let God be true but every man a liar."

The affirmation and act that bids eternal truth be present fact is no dainty, hothouse sort of thing. Present fact can be awfully stubborn, and things as they are look woefully unlike what God says they may be. "A sense of things real comes doubly strong" sometimes. Bidding eternal truth be present fact may seem the wildest of fancies. But all children of Abraham do well to remember that he "hoped against hope" and considered not the impossible.

If present fact looks hopeless and eternal truth seems far removed, remember that Abraham saw them become one because "he believed God."

147

## JULY 13

### MINUS TO PLUS

*Therefore I take pleasure in infirmities, in reproaches, in necessities, in persecutions, in distresses, for Christ's sake: for when I am weak, then am I strong.* II CORINTHIANS 12:10.

PAUL TURNED HIS stumbling-blocks into stepping-stones. John Bunyan in Bedford jail, Fanny Crosby in a prison of blindness "out of weakness were made strong." Long is the list of saints through the ages who have turned minus to plus by the grace of God.

Paul gloried in infirmities. We glory in strength. Paul gloried in tribulation. Most of us grumble. The Christian does not resent his affliction. He does not merely resign himself to it. He rises above it and transmutes it into a blessing. He is "more than conqueror."

This kind of book-keeping turns liabilities into assets. This world cannot understand it. "What things were gain to me, those I counted loss for Christ," says Paul. And then what seems loss he turns to gain!

We hear of people who "lose the savings of a lifetime." But what you really save in a lifetime is what you lay up in heaven, and you cannot lose that. And out of earth's darkest day you can coin heavenly wealth.

Turn your minus to plus!

## JULY 14

### REMEMBER THE HEATHEN!

*Ought ye not to walk in the fear of our God because of the reproach of the heathen our enemies?* NEHEMIAH 5:9.

THE WORLD IS watching us and we ought to walk circumspectly, because the days are evil. Abram and Lot must beware of strife, because the Canaanite and the Perizzite dwell in the land, and "we be brethren" (Gen. 13:7, 8). David's sin gave occasion to the enemies of the Lord to blaspheme (II Sam. 12:14). Paul wrote to Jews, 'The name of God is blasphemed among the Gentiles through you" (Rom. 2:24). Young women are to be taught to live right, "that the word of God be not blasphemed" (Titus 2:5). Peter exhorts believers to a manner of life honest among the Gentiles, "that whereas they speak against you as evil-doers, they may by your good works, which they shall behold, glorify God in the day of visitation" (I Pt. 2:12).

The Canaanite, the Perizzite, the Gentiles live all around us. Lest we bring reproach on the cause we represent we do well to deny ourselves that which may not hurt us but would give occasion to the adversary to blaspheme. The fact that we are free from the law gives us no grounds for foolishly running into license. And God help Abram and Lot and their herdmen to behave before the heathen, for "we be brethren."

JULY 15

"YES, BUT" AND "WHAT IF?"

*Yet I will rejoice in the Lord, I will joy in the God of my salvation.* HABAKKUK 3:18.

HABAKKUK ENUMERATES A lot of gloomy circumstances, failure of figs and olives and vines and fields and flocks. But although these barren states exist, he will rejoice and be glad, for heaven never knows a drought.

Whether actual or potential, we have to reckon with failure around us, and the devil whispers, "Yes, but . . ." and "What if . . .?" "What if you get sick? What if this friend proves false? What if this effort fails?" If you are going to add up all that may happen, you may as well add sleeplessness and maybe a nervous breakdown. And the

149

thing you fear is more than likely to arrive. "I feared a fear and it came upon me" (Job 3:25). We might as well face the worst thing that could happen and say, "Let worse come to worst, so what? I still have God." Drop your tense grip and fall into His arms. Break the tyranny of Yes, But and What If! Faith is worth nothing until it disregards the Failure around us and rejoices in the Faithfulness above us.

## JULY 16

### "TODAY"

*So teach us to number our days, that we may apply our hearts unto wisdom.* PSALM 90:12.

TODAY IS NOT a day to be endured just in order to get over yonder to something better. The grass looks greener in the next pasture, but it is hard to tell which is our most important day. One day has one kind of opportunity, another has another. Let us buy up all the opportunities, for the days are evil.

We are apt to put a red circle around the wrong day. God's calendar does not look like ours. The big day on ours may be without special significance on His. And the ordinary day, when "nothing much happened," may, if redeemed to His glory, be a great day in His sight.

Do not try to evaluate any day, just make the most of it. What seems a dry and tedious interval, a desert stretch between here and yonder, while you burn with a fever to be into the middle of next week, may afford greater opportunity to know God and glorify Him than the glamorous day you are burning to reach.

Besides, this is the only day you can be sure of. "Boast not thyself of tomorrow." And today is the only day of its kind. God never makes two alike. There will never be another day like it. You may call it "just another day," but it isn't. Make it count for God!

150

## ANATHEMA OR MARANATHA?

*If any man love not the Lord Jesus Christ, let him be
Anathema Maranatha.* I Corinthians 16:22.

The great apostle in a day when unbelieving Jews were
calling Jesus accursed throws back the anathema with
power. Then he takes an Aramaic term, which the scholars
have argued over as to whether it means the Lord has
come or "May he come!"

These two words, spelled with almost the same letters,
set forth two viewpoints poles apart. There are millions today whose mark might well be anathema. They blaspheme
the Lord and they are accursed. False preachers of "another Gospel" are anathema. The bitter hostility of long
ago boiled over in that word.

Over against that is the love that said instead, "Jesus is
Lord," and, looking for His return, cried, "Maranatha."
Looking for the Lord was a distinguishing mark of first-
century Christianity. Strange and sad it is that so many who
claim to love Him today do not thrill to "The Lord cometh."

Are you Anathema or Maranatha? Which is the cry of
your soul?

### DON'T MISS JESUS!

*But Thomas . . . was not with them when Jesus came.*
John 20:24.

Thomas missed one meeting of believers and was an unbeliever for a whole week. It pays to be present when Jesus
appears. He guarantees His presence where two or three
gather in His Name. Therefore it pays to be at church.

There are other places where Jesus reveals Himself—the Book and prayer. And He has promised to reveal Himself to those who have His commandments and keep them. The place of obedience—the temple of the willing heart—there you may be sure He appears.

Don't miss Jesus. It makes a doubting Thomas. If we were on hand at these meeting places we would not be demanding extra evidences before we believe. Sometimes our Lord does grant a special manifestation, but "blessed are they that have not seen and yet have believed."

Be there when Jesus comes. I don't know what other business Thomas had that evening, but if your other business makes you miss Jesus you have too much business!

## JULY 19

### "NO OUTSIDE HELP"

*For I was ashamed to require of the king a band of soldiers and horsemen to help us against the enemy in the way: because we had spoken unto the king, saying, The hand of our God is upon all them for good to them that seek him; but his power and his wrath is against all them that forsake him. So we fasted and besought our God for this: and he was intreated of us.*
EZRA 8:22, 23.

EZRA HAD MADE great claims for his God and now he was ashamed to ask assistance from the king. And well we may be, but some of us are not. We recite: "Some trust in chariots and some in horses: but we will remember the name of the Lord our God"; we boast that our God is able to deliver us; but in an emergency we go to Egypt for help or borrow the militia of Artaxerxes. King Asa, after God's mighty deliverance from the Ethiopians, made a league with Syria when Baasha threatened him. Hanani, the seer, said, "Herein hast thou done foolishly." And we always do foolishly when we sing and preach about a God who supplies all our need and then beg help from the ungodly.

It ought to embarrass us to ask help from this world. We do not need its assistance. Let us beseech our God, and He will be entreated of us.

<br>

## JULY 20

### "BEYOND THE CALL OF DUTY"

*We are unprofitable servants: we have done that which was our duty to do.* LUKE 17:10.

HEROES ARE OFTEN decorated for going "above and beyond the call of duty" to perform some feat not required in the ordinary normal course of their obligations. It might shock some church members who pride themselves on doing their duty to be told that they are unprofitable servants, but such we are if we merely do what is normally required of us. Now, it is a good thing to do our duty, and most of us do not even get that far. But we can get that far and merit no better word than "unprofitable." Alas, some of our best church workers and busiest religious folk never get beyond this category.

God's awards are for the Saints of the Second Mile who go above and beyond the call of duty. It is not whipping ourselves up to increased quantity production that is in mind here. It is the spontaneous and overflowing ministry that does far more for Jesus than it has to just because we love Him so.

We are glad to do far more than our duty for those we love on earth. Shall we do less for the Lover of our souls?

153

## "SQUENCHING" THE SPIRIT

*Quench not the Spirit.* I THESSALONIANS 5:19.

A NEGRO FRIEND used to say to me, "Don't 'squench' the Spirit." He coined his own word, but "squench," being a combination of "squelch" and "quench," really should be in the dictionary.

We quench the Spirit in more ways than we suspect. When we stifle the inner impression to speak or act for the Lord we do it. And we can quench the Spirit in others when we criticize or discourage or by any attitude "throw cold water" on their fire. The brother in prayer meeting who mixed his metaphors and said, "Lord, if there should be a spark of fire in this meeting, please water that spark," unwittingly suggested another way to smother the Spirit's freedom. How we do conspire to limit God in our meetings! We have an Honored Guest in every Christian gathering, and He can be grieved very easily. A frivolous spirit, a critical or rebellious frame of mind, a fed-up complacency —that will do it. The very way we arrange physical details, the way we scatter all over the church, two to a pew; the way we hear and hear not—surely "squench" says it, for we squelch and quench the Spirit.

## JULY 22

### REJOICE TODAY!

*This is the day which the Lord hath made; we will rejoice and be glad in it.* PSALM 118:24.

WE LIVE ON retrospect and anticipation. "Yesterday was so wonderful. How we did rejoice and how glad we were in it!" "Tomorrow will be a great day. We will rejoice and be glad then." But today—that is different.

Distance lends enchantment to the view, so yesterday is haloed by the glory of the past. And anticipation does so exceed fulfilment that tomorrow looks better today. Between the two lies *now* and it suffers by comparison.

But true joy is not in days either past or present or to come but in Christ, and He is with us "all the days," as He promised. He is the same yesterday, when we did rejoice. He is the same forever, all the tomorrows, through all eternity, when we shall rejoice. But He is also the same *today*, the day which the Lord hath made. We will be glad and rejoice in it, but better still in *Him*.

## JULY 23

### "THEN THE LORD . . ."

*When my father and my mother forsake me, then the Lord will take me up.* PSALM 27:10.

FROM CHILDHOOD WE like protection and security, someone to turn to. But loved ones fail us in one way or another. Death takes them, distance divides us, other circumstances render them unable to come to our aid. Some know the bitterness of being cast out or deserted by their own people. Precious as is the love and companionship and assistance of our dear ones, we had better not make that our main stay. We can be bereft of them in a moment and forsaken in tragic ways. Sometimes they remain, but because of infirmity cannot help us any more.

But when the choicest companions cannot walk with us, God says, "I will never leave thee nor forsake thee." It was a desolate man, forsaken of one he thought loved him, who penned out of his desperation, "O Love that wilt not let me go." It is well to reckon on the possibility of utter bereavement, of being forsaken by those we hold dearest; but along with it we may count on the promise of never being forsaken by Him who is dearest of all. At the point of darkest human loneliness—*then the Lord*.

## JULY 24

### BE REASONABLE!

*And he thought within himself . . .* LUKE 12:17.
*Why reason ye among yourselves?* MATTHEW 16:8.
*Come now, and let us reason together.* ISAIAH 1:18.

CONTRARY TO THE ideas of some, God does not discourage reason. He wants us to reason with Him. Reasoning within ourselves we arrive at conclusions as wrong as did the rich fool who planned for "many years," when God said, "This night . . ."

Reasoning among ourselves we do no better. The scribes and Pharisees were always reasoning (Mk. 11:31; Lk. 5: 21) but their conclusions led to the crucifying of our Saviour. The disciples reasoned (Mk. 8:17; Lk. 9:46; 24:15), but they reasoned amiss until the Lord cleared things up.

God wants us to reason together with Him on the basis of revelation, not on our poor logic. "The heart has its reasons of which the reason knows nothing," said Pascal. There is a higher logic, which the natural man cannot receive; it is foolishness to him. But if we will let God reason with us, He will reveal His wisdom from above by the Spirit.

"While they . . . reasoned, Jesus himself drew near" (Lk. 24:15). Let Him clear up your problems!

## JULY 25

### THE DIVINE DIAGNOSIS

*These things saith he . . .* REVELATION 2:1.

NOTHING COULD BE clearer than our Lord's dealing with the church at Ephesus, and it is just as fit in our case today. He first commended them for *what they had.* "But this thou

156

hast . . ." He knew their works and labor and patience and their hatred of false doctrine. Our Lord Himself hates the deeds of the Nicolaitanes. Don't forget that. He said so. Then He pointed out *what they did not have.* They had left their first love. You will notice how commendable a church may be and yet be without love. And without that we are but sounding brass and clanging cymbal.

Then Jesus tells them *what to do.* Remember, Repent, Repeat. It is very hard for Ephesus to remember from whence she has fallen. Usually, Ephesus does not think she has had a fall. The books may show a "rise" in membership and financial intake. It is tough going trying to show such churches that they have fallen. And of course repentance and a return to first works are out of the question until Ephesus remembers.

Finally, there is the alternative, *what Christ will do if they obey not.* "Or else . . ." It is revival or removal.

When will we submit to the Divine Diagnosis?

## JULY 26

### PROPER IDENTIFICATION

*Christ liveth in me.* GALATIANS 2:20.

WE ARE ALWAYS intrigued and haunted by the simplicity of first-century Christianity. What would happen if a man started out today to be just a Christian? The idea has inspired books like *In His Steps.* Well, if a man started out to be "just a Christian" he would probably gather a band of "just Christians" around him, and soon there would be another denomination! Through the centuries believers hungry to recapture the simplicity of the early faith have started out to be just friends or disciples or brethren or some other group. But one always has to watch, lest devotion to a group or movement supersede devotion to Christ Himself.

In every Christian Christ lives again. Every true believer is a return to first-century Christianity. The problem is how to maintain the simplicity of being just a Christ-ian, an en-Christed one amid the complexity of the modern religious set-up.

What ought to be most evident in us is that Christ lives in us. If our church or group is more evident than our identification with Christ it is too evident. We are here to advertise Him, not "it" or "us" or "them."

<br>

## JULY 27

### THE CAUSE AND CURE OF ERROR

*Ye do err, not knowing the scriptures, nor the power of God.* MATTHEW 22:29.

FOR ALL OUR education today, we never had more ignorance and error. The root of it is revealed in this word from our Lord: we do not know the Scriptures or the power of God. For Scripture we substitute our own explanations, and for the power of God we substitute our own experience. God has said something to us in the Scriptures, His written Word, and He has done something for us in His Son, the Living Word; but we refuse both and live in error.

Like the generation of Noah's day, this age lives eating and drinking, marrying and giving in marriage, *and knows not,* and will not know until judgment breaks. But God has provided a cure for ignorance. Again and again He says, "I would not have you ignorant" (Rom. 11:25; I Cor. 10:1; 12:1; II Cor. 1:8; I Thess. 4:13; II Pt. 3:8).

The cause of error is plain: ignorance of the Scriptures and of the power of God. The cure is equally plain: knowledge of the Scriptures and of the power of God. The first leads to the second: as we know the Scriptures we may know the power of God. "Faith cometh by hearing, and hearing by the word of God."

## WHEN SELF-DEFENSE IS A SIN

*And he, willing to justify himself, said . . .* LUKE 10:29.

ENDLESS ARE THE devices by which we try to justify our-selves. When Samuel faced Saul returning from battle and disobedient to God, Saul tried to argue the case and ex-plain why he had not exterminated the Amalekites as God had commanded. It is a mark of the disobedient heart to defend itself. David, when confronted by Nathan, did not argue, he broke into the penitence of the Fifty-first Psalm. Saul said, "I have sinned," but true repentance does not substitute sacrifice for obedience. The sacrifice God wants is a broken spirit. David offered that sacrifice, but Saul tried to substitute a burnt-offering.

When the voice of God confronts you with your sin, do not offer God an argument. You cannot justify yourself, anyway. One could finish the text above with dozens of alibis men offer to explain themselves. But when a man really does business with God all arguments and excuses are forgotten in the honest confession, "Against thee, thee only, have I sinned." God justifies freely by His grace, and we are "just-as-if-we'd-never-sinned."

## JULY 29

### STRENGTH FOR THE DAY

*I can do all things through Christ which strengtheneth me.* PHILIPPIANS 4:13.
*As thy days, so shall thy strength be.* DEUTERONOMY 33:25.

RED-LETTER DAYS and lofty experiences tend to fade. Reso-lutions, though penned in blood, soon lose their original drive. Spiritual stimulants, like shots in the arm, may serve a purpose, but living by shots in the arm, whether physically or spiritually, is abnormal. The trolley car does not run all day on one big push of power at the start. Its slender arm reaches up and keeps constant contact with the current.

Christ is our strength and He is with us all the days and is ever available. He will not give us tomorrow's strength today, nor will yesterday's grace suffice. "Sufficient unto the day is the evil thereof," but also sufficient unto the day is the strength thereof with which to meet the evil.

Believe Him for today's strength today!

## JULY 30

### WHAT TO PREACH

*We preach not ourselves, but Christ Jesus the Lord; and ourselves your servants for Jesus' sake.* II CORIN-THIANS 4:5.

HERE IS PROPER orientation for a preacher. He is not to preach himself, his experience, his ideas, his pet themes. The pulpit is no sounding board for a man. He is to preach "Christ Jesus as Lord," the threefold Name so often set forth in Scripture—Messiah, Mediator, Master. "Believe on the Lord Jesus Christ, and thou shalt be saved."

It is a ministry of "Not I but Christ." Where does the preacher come in? "Ourselves your servants for Jesus' sake." Not just servants, period. We are not to be glorified flunkeys waiting on fussy church members. Only that service which is for His sake counts. A lot of things we do and a lot of things people demand are not for Jesus' sake.

But He is the subject of preaching and we are servants. Woe to the man who would make himself the subject and Christ a servant to advance his own ministry!

What to preach? Here is the answer to the old, old question.

160

## TAKING NO CHANCES

*I know whom I have believed.* II TIMOTHY 1:12.

ONCE IN A while somebody speaks of "staking all on Christ," or risking everything on God's promises, as though it were a glorified gamble. But we are not gambling when we venture on God's Word. Staking something on an uncertainty is a gamble, but when we commit to Christ we are depending on an absolute certainty that cannot fail. It is one thing trying to get on by auto-suggestion, trying to imagine what may or may not be actually true. It is another thing venturing on something we know is true, though sometimes it may not be real to us. Then we may with confidence live as though it were true because it is.

God's promises are true, forever settled in heaven. Jesus is true. Heaven and earth shall pass away, but never His words. Paul knew whom he trusted. There is no chance about it, but absolute certainty. We are risking nothing when we trust Him. He will keep the deposit.

## AUGUST 1

## TALK AND WALK

*Are ye not carnal, and walk as men.* I CORINTHIANS 3:3.
*He that saith he abideth in him ought himself also so to walk, even as he walked.* I JOHN 2:6.
*Walk in the Spirit, and ye shall not fulfil the lust of the flesh.* GALATIANS 5:16.

WE ARE TOO much inclined to excuse strife and schism in our churches by saying, "Too err is human; no church is perfect." God has made provision for victory over the flesh, in both the individual and the collective life of His people.

We may have been born the first time with bad tempers, but we have been born again, and the New Adam can conquer the Old. We have no right to accept the miserable divisions and tumults among believers today as though such were a normal condition. It is subnormal and abnormal. If we say we abide in Him we ought to walk as He walked, and we can if we walk in the Spirit.

We are not to walk as men but as saints. "We are all human" is the alibi of backsliders. We have been raised from a human to a heavenly level. If we *say* we abide in Him we ought to *walk* as He walked. Our *walk* should square with our *talk*.


## AUGUST 2

### GOD-THIRSTY

*As the hart panteth after the water brooks, so panteth my soul after thee, O God.* PSALM 42:1.

THERE IS MUCH in our religious life today that is cheap and superficial. There is plenty of glorified big business, wheels within wheels. Men, methods, money, drives and movements and projects are abundant. But, as in other centuries, there are souls here and there who are sick of all that and whose consuming thirst is to know God. Most people are too busy raising quotas and thinking up slogans to walk with God. It takes time to be holy, but who takes time?

It is to be hoped that a new true mysticism will appear and that in this modern bedlam some saints will emerge whose business will be to know God through His Son by His Spirit. We are out to know everything, but never were we more ignorant of God.

God-thirsty souls! "Now Thee alone I seek!" "He satisfieth the longing soul."

162

## "MARVEL NOT . . . IF THE WORLD HATE YOU."

*The world cannot hate you; but me it hateth, because
I testify of it, that the works thereof are evil.* JOHN 7:7.
*If ye were of the world, the world would love his own:
but because ye are not of the world, but I have chosen
you out of the world, therefore the world hateth you.*
JOHN 15:19.

*The world cannot hate you,* said Jesus to His unconverted
brethren. They were of the world and the world loves its
own.

*Me it hateth,* said our Lord of Himself. And why does
it hate Him? "Because I testify of it that the works thereof
are evil." Light has come into the world and men love
darkness rather than light because their deeds are evil.
This world resents the Light that shows it up.

*The world hateth you,* said our Lord to His disciples.
And why does the world hate us? "Because ye are not of
the world, but I have chosen you out of the world." As we
testify of the world that its deeds are evil and as we let our
light shine and expose the unfruitful works of darkness,
we share the hatred this age feels toward our Lord.

"The world knoweth us not, because it knew him not"
(I Jno. 3:1).

## AUGUST 4

### TOO BUSY

*As thy servant was busy here and there, he was gone.*
I KINGS 20:40.

THE MAN IN this story received a charge to keep, but he
was unfaithful, not because he was lazy or asleep, but because he was too busy. Idleness may be the devil's work-

shop, but so is busyness if we are so busy that the best thing gets away.

Parents are too busy, and the children get away. Christians are too busy even with good things, and the best thing—to know God—gets away. Preachers are too busy, and the devotional life is lost. And while we are puttering life gets away.

The day of grace, the accepted time of salvation, passes unredeemed because we are too busy with the here and there and so forget the eternal.

If you are too busy to find time for God, you are too busy. You have received a charge to keep, and if your busyness keeps you from being about your Father's business, you are a poor business man!

## AUGUST 5

### TAKEN OUT OR TAKEN THROUGH?

*I pray not that thou shouldest take them out of the world, but that thou shouldest keep them from the evil.*
JOHN 17:15.

HOW OFTEN HAVE parents wished that they might keep their children pure and innocent, and how much they have dreaded what this wicked world might do to them. Saints in the Middle Ages tried to escape from the world to pursue a holy life in some secluded retreat. But we are not kept from evil that way. The defense must be from within. Indeed, we must shun every worldly force and influence that lowers our resistance to sin, but we have to live in this world, though we are not of it, and we can be kept from evil in the midst of it. We cannot run from this present world nor hide in a cave from the madding crowd's ignoble strife. We have to make our way through it all, but we can be kept by the power of God.

The boat can be in the water without the water being in the boat. Lord, do not take us *out* of the world, take us *through!*

## AUGUST 6

### "NOTWITHSTANDING THE LORD . . ." . . . .

*At my first answer no man stood with me, but all men forsook me. . . . Notwithstanding the Lord stood with me, and strengthened me.* II TIMOTHY 4:16, 17.

PAUL MENTIONS THE failure of men, but he majors on the faithfulness of God. We had better learn early to put no confidence in the flesh—in ourselves or in others. Our most familiar friend, which did eat of our bread, may lift up his heel against us. Our Lord's disciples forsook Him and fled. Paul is tasting the same bitter experience. In his loneliness he begs Timothy to "come before winter."

We can easily grow wretched over the failure of men, even the best of them. There is so much fickleness and so many Christians fail us. We had better resolve early to expect little of men, much of God. Major on His faithfulness! We have His promise and we may be sure of His presence, for the one assures the other.

Raise your sights higher than men. Then, if even your father and mother forsake you, the Lord will take you up.

## AUGUST 7

### PLEASING GOD

*I do always those things that please him.* JOHN 8:29.

WE LIVE TO please someone, ourselves, other people or God. Jesus "pleased not himself" (Rom. 15:3). We are not to live to please men. "Do I seek to please men?" (Gal. 1: 10). "Not as pleasing men but God" (I Thess. 2:4). We are to please our neighbor for his good to edification (Rom. 15:2). Paul said he pleased all men, seeking, not his profit, but theirs, that they might be saved (I Cor. 10:33).

We are to please God, as our Lord said in our text. God was pleased in His Son (Mt. 3:17). He was not pleased with the Israelites in the wilderness (I Cor. 10:5). We had better take warning from them, for "these things happened unto us for ensamples." Enoch pleased God (Heb. 11:5). We cannot please God in the flesh (Rom. 8:8). It is impossible without faith (Heb. 11:6). But as we submit to God He works in us to will and to do of *His good pleasure* (Phil. 2:13). Then we are to live so as to please Him who hath chosen us to be soldiers (II Tim. 2:3, 4). And if we please Him we get answers to our prayers (I Jno. 3:22).

Whom are you living to please?

## AUGUST 8

### ALONE, YET NOT ALONE

*Behold, the hour cometh, yea, is now come, that ye shall be scattered every man to his own, and shall leave me alone: and yet I am not alone, because the Father is with me.* JOHN 16:32.

BLESSED PARADOX OF the Saviour and the Saint! Our Lord was a solitary soul, yet not alone. And the Christian who presses into the deeper things of God will often be lonely but never alone. Paul was lonely in the Roman prison: "All men forsook me." But he was not alone: "The Lord stood with me."

"He that sent me is with me: the Father hath not left me alone." Jacob may fancy himself alone in a strange land,

166

with a stone for a pillow, but he will make a discovery: "Surely the Lord is in this place and I knew it not."

Live as though He were with you, for He is. You have His word for it and you can be confident of His promise, though you may not be conscious of His presence.

Even through the Valley of Death's Shadow, "I will fear no evil, *FOR THOU ART WITH ME.*" Alone yet not alone!

## AUGUST 9

### DOING BUSINESS WITH CHRIST: DEMONS

*What have we to do with thee, Jesus, thou Son of God?*
MATTHEW 8:29.

THE DEVIL AND the world of demons must face Christ. The devil tried to do business with Him, but the Lord dismissed him: "Get thee hence, Satan." The devil is not in the first two chapters of the Bible or in the last two. Thank God for a Book that disposes of the devil!

There is no concord between Christ and Belial. The demons cried, "Art thou come to torment us *before the time?*" They are doomed to the lake of fire prepared for the devil and his angels. They are overactive today because their time is short. The only power that can control them is Christ. Much that goes by other names today is really the work of the powers of darkness. And note that they know Jesus is the Son of God, a fact which many poor humans will not accept.

Our Lord has no traffic with the world of demons. There is no ground where they can get together. Let us beware of doing business with the devil. And if you don't want to trade with him, stay out of his shops!

## AUGUST 10

### DOING BUSINESS WITH CHRIST: PILATE

*What shall I do then with Jesus which is called Christ?*
MATTHEW 27:22.

PILATE HAD TO do business with Jesus, and so must we all.
We cannot wash our hands of the whole business any more
than could he. We cannot leave Christ alone. The question
is not, "What will you do with Jesus?" but "What are you
doing with Him now?" We are for or against, we gather
with Him or we scatter abroad.

Pilate faced the alternatives of cynicism: "What is
truth?"; criminality: "Barabbas or Jesus?"; Cæsar: "If thou
let this man go thou art not Cæsar's friend." The issue is always "Christ or . . . .'

This unbelieving world, whether it choose the cynic, the
criminal, or Cæsar, must do something with Christ. He is
inescapable. And men must settle with Christ, not with a
church or a preacher. Let us never obscure the issue: what
are you doing with Jesus the Christ? "He that believeth on
him is not condemned: but he that believeth not is condemned already, because he hath not believed in the name
of the only begotten Son of God."

### AUGUST 11

### DOING BUSINESS WITH CHRIST:
### THE YOUNG RULER

*Good Master, what good thing shall I do, that I may
have eternal life?* MATTHEW 19:16.

THIS PROMISING YOUTH did no real business with Jesus, because he did not really mean business. For all his manners
and morals and money, he would not pay the price of real

168

discipleship. Some very nice people would like to have eternal life as a good investment, but Jesus is not handing out salvation in return for another "good thing" on our self-righteous record of commandments already kept. He wanted to blast this young ruler into a real venture of daring faith that would cut him loose from his security, but the prospective disciple would not move from his moorings. It turned out that, after all, he loved his money more than his soul.

It takes a radical break to turn a man from earth's trash to heaven's treasure. Our Lord came immediately to the issue and would have this young man cut the knot instead of gradually untying it. He would have him bring the matter to a quick climax and be done with it.

For all his good points, this fine prospect missed his blessing while poorer specimens like Bartimæus, Zacchæus, the Samaritan woman, got theirs. Jesus loved him, but lost him because the questioner never meant business, though no man ever seemed to mean business more than he.

## AUGUST 12

### DOING BUSINESS WITH CHRIST: PAUL

*Who art thou, Lord? . . . Lord, what wilt thou have me
to do?* Acts. 9:5, 6.

PAUL DID BUSINESS with the Lord. His was the authentic Who-What experience. Men who mean business with the Lord are definite and practical: "What comes next? What shall I do now?" Whatsoever He says, they do.

We live in a slovenly age, when duty and obedience and discipline have been relegated to the attic, along with the worn-out parlor lamp and cylinder-record phonograph. We had better bring them downstairs. We are not doing too well without them. A generation of unconverted young

169

Sauls kicks against the pricks. They will not do business with Christ, because to do so He must be confessed and obeyed as Lord. "Who, Lord? Lord, what?" A lot of sentimental slush about Jesus forgets that "love so amazing, so divine, *demands* my soul, my life, my all."

The young ruler refused to submit to the Lordship of Jesus. Paul started right: "Who, Lord? Lord, what?" And who ever did greater business with and for His Lord?


## AUGUST 13

### HOW GOOD WERE "THE GOOD OLD DAYS"?

*Say not thou, What is the cause that the former days were better than these? for thou dost not inquire wisely concerning this.* ECCLESIASTES 7:10.

"DISTANCE LENDS ENCHANTMENT to the view," and in retrospect we crown the past with a halo. Like Saul, we try to call up Samuel, and sigh, "If only Wesley or Finney or Moody were alive now!" Elisha did not pine for Elijah: he asked, "Where is the Lord God of Elijah?"

Someone wrote to an editor, saying, "Your paper is not as good as it used to be." He replied, "It never has been."

Some of the old worthies could take pretty mean cracks at each other. If you go all the way back to the Early Church, consider the plight of Corinth. And even in Acts it was not long after Pentecost that "there arose a murmuring."

We do not inquire wisely when we cast longing eyes in the direction of the past. The days of Elijah are gone but the God of Elijah lives today. There are no untarnished haloes in any generation, and looking at heroes of any era is disappointing. Look not to "the good old days" but to the God of all the days.

## AUGUST 14

### WE ASKED FOR IT

*Hast thou not procured this unto thyself, in that thou hast forsaken the Lord thy God, when he led thee by the way?* JEREMIAH 2:17.
*Are not these evils come upon us because our God is not among us?* DEUTERONOMY 31:17.

OUR PLIGHT TODAY is our own fault. We asked for it. All our modern evils are come upon us because God is not among us. Of course, He is omnipresent, but He is not among us in that we have not His favor, the smile of His approval.

God has been among us in blessings unnumbered, but we have forgotten Him. And to be lost it is not necessary for a nation to blaspheme God. "The wicked shall be cast into hell and all nations that *forget* God."

Even God's people sometimes ask, "Is the Lord among us or not?" And in the absence of Him we are faced with the presence of evils galore.

We have lost the sense of God in the nation, in the churches, in our lives. The biggest business of the hour is to draw nigh to God that He may draw nigh to us. His presence with us is too often an assumption in our heads instead of an awareness in our hearts.


## AUGUST 15

### PERSONALIZING THE PROGRAM

*Ye shall be witnesses unto me.* ACTS 1:8.

WHAT WE SAY is a witness, too, but people are moved by the living witness as well as by the spoken testimony. It is slow business getting a congregation warmed up to a mis-

171

sionary program. But let a real live Spirit-filled missionary embody that program and see the difference! We have degenerated into money-raisers for a project or a budget, and what a weariness it is! "Next Sunday we must raise an offering for the orphanage, the church paper, the college." The causes of Christ do not strike fire until we incarnate them. Dutifully soliciting funds for a church enterprise is hard going. One orphan can be more eloquent than an hour's speech about the orphanage.

Christianity suffers today because it has become merely a big business in the minds of some and now we must raise the funds to keep the business going. It goes best when it is embodied in flaming witnesses. Christ is a Person, and He reaches other persons through persons, not merely through plans and propaganda. We are propagandizing the faith instead of propagating it.

## AUGUST 16

### THE CONSTRAINT OF CHRIST

*We love him, because he first loved us.* I JOHN 4:19. *For ye know the grace of our Lord Jesus Christ that, though he was rich, yet for your sakes he became poor, that ye through his poverty might be rich.* II CORINTHIANS 8:9.

CHRIST IS THE true motivation of Christian conduct. We do not love Him because we ought but because love begets love. He loved us and our hearts respond. We love others because His love constrains us, because the love of God is shed abroad in our hearts by the Holy Ghost.

Likewise, we give, not because we ought and not because of the need primarily, but because He gave. "Jesus paid it all, all to Him I owe." Freely we have received, freely we give. Not grudgingly or of necessity, but cheerfully. Witness a drive for church funds, a pitiful plea on Sunday to wangle a few dollars of "church dues" and you will perceive how far we have left the New Testament way. The stunts, picnics, bazaars, the moth-eaten jokes, the high-pressure—"Who'll give ten dollars?" God forgive us! God will never accept such money wrung from church misers. It is the gift without the giver, a vain oblation.

## AUGUST 17

### LACKING "ONE THING" OR "NOTHING"

*Lacked ye anything?* LUKE 22:35.
*One thing thou lackest.* MARK 10:21.

WHEN THE DISCIPLES went forth at the bidding of Jesus without purse or scrip or shoes, they lacked nothing. The rich young ruler had purse and scrip and shoes, but when he went away he lacked one thing, and, lacking that, he lacked everything.

When we obey our Lord's orders and go forth by His commission we find His grace sufficient and our needs supplied through God's riches in glory by Christ Jesus. But a man may have all else, yet if he be not willing to abandon it all for the Master, he is a pauper. The supreme thing in this life is to count all things but loss for the excellency of the knowledge of Christ Jesus the Lord. A man may have kept other commandments, but if he will not cut loose from his dearest earthly treasure at the bidding of the Lord, he has failed at the vital point and is still a rebel.

Nothing matters but this: does Jesus have the utter ab- solute first and final say in your life? If He does, you will lack nothing.

## JESUS MADE REAL

*He shall glorify me: for he shall receive of mine and shall shew it unto you.* JOHN 16:14.

WE DO NOT make Jesus real by conjuring up a mental picture of Him long ago in Galilee and trying to walk in imagination with Him there. We do not have to go back two thousand years or travel to Palestine to find Jesus. There is a fad for that sort of thing, but so might one inwardly visualize any character of history. Such mental association may, indeed, affect one's life to some degree, but it is far from the way Christ is made real to the believer.

The Holy Spirit has come for that purpose. All things spiritual are *from* God *through* Christ and are communicated to us *by* the Spirit. It was expedient that Jesus should go that the Spirit might come. He does not testify of Himself but of Christ, and He makes the Lord real to the heart. It is not a mere mental exercise but the work of the Spirit that enables us to say, "He is real to me."

## AUGUST 19

## TAKE HIS WORD FOR IT

*Let God be true, but every man a liar.* ROMANS 3:4.

"ABRAHAM BELIEVED GOD." The essence of faith is simply taking God at His Word. "What more can he say than to you he hath said?" "He hath said . . . so that we may boldly say." We are thrown back upon revelation, not reason. God has spoken and holy men recorded it. Back of everything stands the record. If we are to believe the Living Word we must accept the Written Word. Jesus accepted the Old Testament as the Word of God. And He told us that His words were spirit and life. "Tis so sweet to trust in Jesus"—but how do we trust Him? The next line has it, "Just to take Him at His word."

Not "a feeling fond and fugitive," not a frame of mind strenuously maintained, but a calm reliance on, "It is written," that is it. For "these are written, that ye might believe that Jesus is the Christ, the Son of God: and that believing ye might have life through his name."

Take His Word for it!

## AUGUST 20

### LOVE AND LABOR

*Lovest thou me? . . . Feed my sheep.* JOHN 21:16.

OUR LORD JOINS love and labor. Our service for Him is a "labor of love" (I Thess. 1:3), a labor growing out of love. We should feed not only the sheep He has, but other sheep that He seeks we should help to bring into the fold.

Our Lord never thought of relationship to Him that does not issue in fruitfulness for Him. If we abide in Him we shall bring forth much fruit (Jno. 15:5). He that is with Him gathers with Him. He had no thought of fellowship without fruitfulness. We are married to Another, that we might bring forth fruit unto God (Rom. 7:4).

There is no place in Scripture for this type of church member who sings, "O How I Love Jesus," but feeds no sheep; who sings, "Rescue The Perishing," but does no rescue work himself.

"He that hath my commandments and keepeth them, he it is that loveth me." "Follow me and I will make you fishers of men." Because we love we labor.

175

## ISHMAEL AND ISAAC

*Abraham had two sons, the one by a bondmaid, the other by a freewoman. But he who was of the bondwoman was born after the flesh; but he of the freewoman was by promise.* GALATIANS 4:22, 23.

ISHMAEL WAS THE result of a resort to the flesh, proposed by Sarai when God had already promised a son by her. To this day Ishmael and Isaac war in Arab and Jew. Any scheme of our own that takes matters in our own hands when God has spoken otherwise leads to plenty of trouble.

How many today live with war in their hearts because that which is of the flesh contends with that which is of faith! Call it inhibitions, complexes, neuroses, dress it up in psychiatric verbiage, it is but Ishmael and Isaac warring in the soul.

Abraham gave up Ishmael and he never returned. He gave up Isaac but God returned him. Give God your Ishmael—all that is of the flesh—that it may not return. Give Him Isaac too—that which is of faith—that He may return it sanctified and meet for the Master's use.

### AUGUST 22

## OUR COMING INHERITANCE

*The wealth of the sinner is laid up for the just.* PROVERBS 13:22.

"THE MEEK SHALL inherit the earth." Somebody has said, "That is the only way they'll get it." But true it is that the saints shall live and reign with Christ, and all the wealth that sinners have accumulated will eventually pass under the jurisdiction of the righteous. We can afford to wait. The wisest of wealthy kings wrote: "For God giveth to a man that is good in his sight wisdom, and knowledge, and joy: but to the sinner he giveth travail, to gather and to heap up, that he may give it to him that is good before God" (Ecc. 2:26). "The earth is the Lord's and the fulness thereof," and everything comes back eventually to its owner and His people. Men have their transient leases and enjoy the earth for a season, but all the wealth they gather will end up finally in the coffers of the just. The meek may serve in humble station now, but they shall come into their own. Why try to buy up so much earth now, when we shall inherit it later?

## AUGUST 23

### "IT" OR "HIM"?

*I am the resurrection and the life.* JOHN 11:25.

MARTHA BELIEVED IN the resurrection, but Jesus moved her from the doctrinal to the personal: "I am the resurrection." The resurrection is not an "It"—"I am the resurrection." We stop too often with "It." We get an idea, a theory, a doctrine in our heads, but we do not get Him in our hearts. We go in for sanctification, the victorious life, the second coming, and we believe and preach them with a vengeance, but we do not find our hearts warmed—we have "It," not Him. We seek this blessing and that, we join this group and that, we think, "Now I have found *it*," but all that is true and all that we need is in *Him*. We can even major on prayer and faith and not get through to *Him*. We can search the Scriptures and not come to Him that we might have life.

There is no life in any *It*, however good. *He* is our life. In *Him* all things—including all the "Its"—consist.

177

## AUGUST 24

### CAMPAIGN AGAINST RAMOTH-GILEAD

*Shouldest thou help the ungodly, and love them that
hate the Lord?* II CHRONICLES 19:2.

JEHOSHAPHAT WAS A good man, but he allowed himself to be
persuaded by Ahab to join him in an expedition against
Ramoth-gilead. They called in the prophets after the decision already had been made in order to get their blessing,
just as we often make our plans and then ask God to bless
them instead of asking God for a plan. All the sycophant
prophets concurred, except Micaiah, who told them the
truth and was put in prison and fed the bread and water of
affliction. The expedition resulted in Ahab's death. Then
Jehu reproved Jehoshaphat with the words of our text.

God never wants His people to team up with the ungodly in their ventures. We have a different program and
there is no concord between Christ and Belial. Ahab is always going up against some Ramoth-gilead, and all it takes,
as in this case, is a big supper to line up unwise Jehosha-
phats. Better a Micaiah on bread and water than a Jehoshaphat at a banquet, when a Ramoth-gilead campaign is
brewing.

## AUGUST 25

### "I WOULD HAVE TOLD YOU"

*In my Father's house are many mansions: if it were not
so, I would have told you.* JOHN 14:2.

HERE IS A blessed little word often overlooked: "If it were
not so, I would have told you." Jesus not only affirms posi-
tively the glorious fact of our heavenly home, He makes it
doubly sure by a negative: "If it were not so, I would have
told you."

Countless multitudes have wondered whether there is a home beyond. Here is One who came from there and knows. We can take His word for it. He affirms it. And, furthermore, He assures us that if there were no such place He would have told us. He would not leave us in the dark. If death ends all He would have said so. But He died and returned to prove that the best is yet to come. And why do we wonder and hope, when we can know about our future dwelling-place? He would have let us know if there were no such abode. And He did let us know that there is!

I am not left merely to guess about it and hope for the best. I have a double guarantee: "There are many mansions: if there were not, I would have told you."

## AUGUST 26
### DOCTRINE, DYNAMIC, DISCIPLINE

*Take heed unto thyself, and unto the doctrine.* I TIMOTHY 4:16.
*Stir up the gift of God which is in thee.* II TIMOTHY 1:6.
*Thou therefore endure hardness, as a good soldier of Jesus Christ.* II TIMOTHY 2:3.

DOCTRINE, DYNAMIC, DISCIPLINE—Paul would have young Timothy qualified in all three. For lack of any or all, our Timothys do not fare so well today. Some know not what they believe or else turn from truth to fable. Some lack fire from heaven, vainly "compassing themselves about with sparks." And real discipleship has given way to a modern version without a cross.

How the church suffers for lack of all three! How many members can give a reason for their hope? How much of our religious activity is the work of the Spirit? And while we have professed believers aplenty, how many disciples do we have?

We need a fresh course in the Three D's!

179

## AUGUST 27

### CONFIDENCE AND CARE

*Casting all your care upon him; for he careth for you.*
I Peter 5:7.
*Cast not away therefore your confidence, which hath great recompense of reward.* Hebrews 10:35.

ALAS, WE REVERSE the process: we cast away our confidence and carry all our care! It is His desire that we roll all our burden on Him and be careful for nothing. But we are so cumbered with ourselves that our minds are never free to be occupied with Him. If we can let Him take care of our problems while we attend to His work, we shall find our hearts free from that friction that cuts down our service to such a bare minimum. We get so little done for Him, our production is so pitiful, because everything goes into "overhead" and oiling the machinery. Most of our time and energy go into carrying what God asked us to cast on Him. And our confidence, the one thing He said to keep, we cast away.

You keep your confidence: He'll keep your cares!

## AUGUST 28

### "JESUS, MASTER"

*If thou shalt confess with thy mouth Jesus as Lord . . .*
Romans 10:9.

IN HIS *Journal,* John Wesley tells us that, a few days after Aldersgate, he awoke with "Jesus, Master" in his heart and in his mouth. The true believer acknowledges Jesus not only as His Saviour but as Lord of his life. We have a strange species of believer these days, a believer who confesses Christ as Saviour but whose life rejects Him as Master. The New Testament presents no such anomaly as a

180

Christian who "takes" Christ now for salvation and defers obeying Him as Lord until later, maybe never. The initial confession set forth in our text is "Jesus *As Lord*."

If this were made clear to our "prospects" these days, and if they understood that a believer is also expected to be a disciple and a witness, it might drive away some, but we would not be embarrassed by a host of church members who call Him Lord, Lord, and do not His commandments.

John Wesley started right with "Jesus, Master" in His heart as well as in his mouth.

## AUGUST 29

### KNOWN AND UNKNOWN

*The world knoweth us not, because it knew him not.*
I JOHN 3:1.
*I never knew you.* MATTHEW 7:23.

THIS WORLD KNEW not our Lord. "There standeth one among you whom ye know not." So said John the Baptist. "If thou hadst known . . . If thou knewest . . . If ye had known"—so runs Jesus' constant refrain while He was among us.

Because the world knew Him not it knows us not. "Marvel not, my brethren, if the world hate you" (I Jno. 3:13). It not only does not know us, it hates us. "I have given them thy word; and the world hath hated them" (Jno. 17:14). We cannot love the Word and be loved by the world.

But what matters the hatred of this world if He knows and loves us? Most fearful of all pronouncements ever to fall on human ears is that word to those who profess to know Him but whose works deny Him: "I never knew you."

"The Lord knoweth them that are his" (II Tim. 2:19). This world makes much of "knowing the right people." What matters is to know God.

181

## HERE OR HEREAFTER?

*A crown . . . unto all them also that love his appearing.
. . . Demas hath forsaken me, having loved this present
world.* II TIMOTHY 4:8, 10.

IF YOU LOVE His appearing you are not in love with this present world. "If any man love the world, the love of the Father is not in him." "Whosoever therefore will be a friend of the world is the enemy of God."

Paul had set his sights higher than this passing scene. Demas would have his portion here and now. Paul was a pilgrim and a stranger, not only in love with Jesus but with His appearing. I wonder how many really love Jesus' return. One does not sense it much in churches building the Kingdom but not really joying in the coming of the King. And fundamentalists who revel in detailed programs of that event do not always seem to "love" it. Their interest is academic but not affectionate.

Demas sometimes lines up with Paul temporarily, but soon forsakes him. You cannot love and live for two worlds at a time. The love of the world and the love of the Father simply do not coexist in the same heart.

Are you in love with this age or with the one to come? It makes a difference!

## AUGUST 31

### "BUT GOD WAS WITH HIM"

*But God was with him.* ACTS 7:9.

THIS IS ONE of the many "But Gods" in the Book that spell quite a difference. Joseph's brothers sold him into Egypt, *but God was with him.* Joseph himself put it this way: "Ye thought evil against me; but God meant it unto good" (Gen. 50:20). What men *thought* was overruled by what God *wrought.* "Man proposes but God disposes."

"He hath said, I will never leave thee, nor forsake thee. So that we may boldly say, The Lord is my helper, and I will not fear what man shall do unto me" (Heb. 13:5, 6). No plottings of men, no combinations of circumstances can defeat the man who has God as his helper. Here is the secret of many a life, conspired against by ill health, poverty, evil men, foes in the household, the world, the flesh and the devil, but victorious, anyway—*God was with him.* The devil and men often overstep themselves, sell Joseph into Egypt, but God makes him Prime Minister! "If God be for us, who can be against us?"

And even in the last dark chapter we need not tremble at our Adversary, but triumph with our Ally—"I will fear no evil, *for thou art with me.*"

*But God was with him.* What a difference that makes!


### SEPTEMBER 1

#### SECOND CHILDHOOD

*Except ye be converted and become as little children, ye shall not enter into the kingdom of heaven.* MAT-THEW 18:3.

THE CRYING NEED with most of us is not so much to learn more as to unlearn much of what we already know. We know too much. We are cluttered with a mental attic full of things we have read and heard, and now we need to get through—not back—to a few elementary simplicities. There is a second childhood, not of childishness but of childlikeness. To reach it requires a conversion, maybe a sort of

183

second conversion with some of us, when we become just simple Christians content to trust and obey. Some great scholars as well as plain souls reach it. It is not a peak so high that only a few rarely endowed climbers can scale it; it is a valley so low that only a few will humble themselves to walk in it. We are straining too hard trying to be profound and deep to let go and be children again in spirit. And we get there heart first, not head first.

## DOUBLE ABUNDANCE

*God is able to make all grace abound toward you; that ye, always having all sufficiency in all things, may abound to every good work.* II Corinthians 9:8.

God's grace is not only amazing grace, it is abounding grace. He abounds toward us that we may abound toward Him. There is abundance of grace in order that there may be abundance of good works. "Always having all sufficiency in all things"—what could be more satisfying than that? It is another way of saying, "My grace is sufficient for thee." There is nothing stingy and niggardly about the grace of God. "Of his fulness have all we received and grace upon grace." Jesus came that we might have life more abundantly.

And as God abounds toward us, we should abound toward Him. Paul was a great example of what he wrote. With all his infirmities, his thorn in the flesh, his opposition and persecution, who ever abounded to every good work as he did?

Our penurious and miserly service today declares that we live cheaply in our souls. We do not lay hold of the riches of grace in Christ Jesus. Our output is small because our intake is small. "My God shall supply all your need," and beyond that do more for us than we can ask or think. Let us be doubly abundant, in grace and good works.

## SEPTEMBER 3

### "BY HEART" OR "BY HEARSAY"?

*Now we believe, not because of thy saying: for we have heard him ourselves, and know that this is indeed the Christ, the Saviour of the world. JOHN 4:42.*

THE SAMARITANS "BELIEVED" (v. 39), and now they knew the Saviour "by heart," for themselves. There is a second-hand, by-proxy knowledge of the Lord as a report but not as a reality. Andrew and Philip were not content for Peter and Nathanael to know Jesus by hearsay, they brought Peter and Nathanael to the Lord Himself. We have heard and believed the report of Him, and we must, for "faith cometh by hearing and hearing by the word of God." But how many in our churches have had a personal encounter with the Saviour?

The Samaritan woman, like Philip, said, "Come and see." Much of our personal work, our Sunday-school teaching, our preaching, falls short of that. We disseminate information about Jesus, but we often fail to clinch the matter by bringing men and women into His presence. True, they cannot see Him as the Samaritans saw Him. But they can believe on Him and know Him "by heart," as they did.

And how often is the "deeper Christian life," or whatever you may call it, hearsay? We have heard it in a sermon, read it in a book; but that is all. Job knew it "by heart," not hearsay, when he cried: "I have heard of thee by the hearing of the ear but now mine eye seeth thee."

185

## THE BEST PROMOTER

*Promotion cometh neither from the east, nor from the west, nor from the south. But God is the judge: he putteth down one, and setteth up another.* PSALM 75: 6, 7.

PROMOTION IN THIS world is by no means based on merit. Not even in the religious world. Some of the best preachers hold forth in obscure places, while some who cannot and never will preach occupy important pulpits.

God's system of promotion does not follow the pattern of this age. It may look like anything but promotion, as when the Spirit sent Philip out of a spiritual awakening into a desert. God "hides" some of His best talent in unknown corners and buries some of His ablest servants in the depths of heathenism. He seems to waste some of His choicest men. They get scant recognition in this scrambled church world today, where servants ride on horses and princes walk as servants. Today, as ever, the prophet walks in the steps of his Lord, without honor in his own country.

It comes to this: which kind of promotion do we seek? A smart politician who knows the "right" people can attain to considerable eminence down here. But the man who lets God promote him is spared all that fever. God may set him in a high place to the chagrin of some of his contemporaries. If he never gets a newspaper headline he will lose no sleep over it, for any place is a "large place" if it is God's place.

### BETWEEN YESTERDAY AND TOMORROW

*Our fathers worshipped in this mountain. . . . I know that Messias cometh.* JOHN 4:20, 25.

THE SAMARITAN WOMAN was living between a golden past and a glorious future, but in a bleak and sinful present.

She could look back to great days, when her fathers worshiped God, and to greater days ahead, when Messias would come and tell all things. Yet how little did she know that morning that this day would be her greatest, for then she would come to see and know the Master for herself!

How many of us live looking back or ahead, between a holy past and a holier future, but in a hollow present! Some sigh for the good old days when our fathers worshiped in this mountain. Some long for a better day ahead, when the Great Avenger shall vindicate us of our adversaries. But we need not stand at Jacob's well with our souls unsatisfied. The Messiah has come, He lives today, and He will meet us now where we are and as we are. We cannot go back to the fountains of yesterday nor drink at the springs of tomorrow. But the Living Christ offers living water today which shall be in us a well of water springing up into everlasting life. And we shall leave our old waterpots which we would fain have filled at earth's broken cisterns to tell others what we have found in Him today.

### SEPTEMBER 6

### LOOKING UP

*Neither know we what to do: but our eyes are upon thee.* II CHRONICLES 20:12.

JEHOSHAPHAT IS FACED by a powerful combination of Moabites, Ammonites, and others. In his desperation he turns to God: "O God, wilt thou not judge them? for we have no might against this great company that cometh against us."

Are we not often in this plight? Do these lines fall under the eye of someone sore beset by an alliance of evil confederates, whether in the flesh or of the unseen world of

187

principalities and powers? You do not know what to do. We never do. We have no might against the Moabites.

But we can take Jehoshaphat's way out: "Our eyes are upon thee." We may not know what to do, but God always knows what He is going to do. He is never caught off guard or taken by surprise. Commit your case to Him. You can lie down at night and sleep, although tomorrow the Moabites will arrive. Many a saint has pillowed his head on a promise when all hope seemed gone. And when the dreaded day arrived God had handled the Moabites in His own way.

"Our eyes are upon thee." "Looking unto Jesus." We know not what to do, but He knows. No sleeping pill can rest a man like knowing that!

## SEPTEMBER 7

### "PLACING" JUDAS

*Judas by transgression fell, that he might go to his own place.* ACTS 1:25.

JUDAS WAS OUT of place as an apostle. The other eleven may not have known it, but Jesus was not deceived. "Have not I chosen you twelve, and one of you is a devil?" "He knew what was in man." Judas kept up the pretense for several years, and was even treasurer of the twelve. But one day the farce ended and his real self came out, and he ended up where he belonged.

Men always ultimately arrive at their own place. They may be deacons or even stand in pulpits and deceive the people. But there are prepared places for prepared people. There are dwelling-places our Saviour has prepared for His own. There is a lake of fire prepared for the devil and his angels. And Judas arrives in time at his proper destination.

188

Many a Judas out of place goes to great pains to "belong." He tries to act naturally in the church and pose as a Christian. But the Lord knoweth them that are His, and all others, including some who may have prophesied in His day, must one day depart—for Judas belongs to another place.

## SEPTEMBER 8

### THREE WORLDS

*The world that then was . . .*
*The heavens and earth, which are now . . .*
*Nevertheless, we . . . look for new heavens and a new*
*earth.* II PETER 3:6, 7, 13.

WE ARE HEARING much about "one world." The Christian thinks in terms of three worlds. The first was destroyed by water. The second will perish by fire. The believer looks for a third, where righteousness dwells. This present world is reserved for fire. The new world is reserved for us who have become citizens of heaven, to whom this present evil world is but our passage, not our portion. We are strangers and pilgrims, we seek a city.

The people of the first world "knew not" until the flood came. Only Noah had his eyes open. The people of our world know not, nor will they know, until sudden destruction comes. They pride themselves on what they know, but it is only educated ignorance. There are those today, however, like Noah who know what time of day it is. When the last storm begins to break and all heads in this world droop, they will lift up theirs, for redemption nears. The Third World is about to begin!

189

## SEPTEMBER 9

### THE BELOVED UNSEEN

*Whom having not seen, ye love.* I PETER 1:8.

WALKING WITH A little four-year-old, I said something
about loving Jesus. "But how can I love Him," she asked,
"when I can't see Him?"

Thus she posed a problem which has occupied not a few
grown-ups. Peter had seen Jesus. He was writing to Christians who had not. Yet they loved Him, anyway, and
though now they saw Him not, *yet believing*, they rejoiced
with joy unspeakable and full of glory.

We cannot see Him, but He lives and we can believe.
And if we trust Him the Spirit makes Him real and the
love of God is shed abroad in our hearts. And we make our
way through this evil world in love with One we have never
seen. We are not infatuated with a hero of fiction, a memory
or an ideal. We love a Living Person who was and is, and
we shall be like Him, for one day we shall see Him as He is.

Yes, we can love Him though we cannot see Him.


## SEPTEMBER 10

### WOUNDED AFRESH

*What are these wounds in thine hands? . . . These with
which I was wounded in the house of my friends.*
ZECHARIAH 13:6.

OUR LORD'S MOST grievous wounds are suffered at the hands
of professing Christians, those who claim to be His friends.
Judas was not the only man who has betrayed Jesus, nor
is Peter the sole disciple who has denied Him. He is daily
crucified afresh by those who call Him Lord, Lord, and
do not His commands.

190

The present-day dens of iniquity, the liquor shops, theaters, the card playing and gambling, all the big, booming business of sin would practically be out of business if all church members withdrew their support. Staggering bums in the gutters are of little value to the devil. He prizes most the men and women who wear the livery of saints and live the lives of sinners.

Indeed, our Lord is wounded by this foul and blasphemous world. But His deepest scars He gets at the hands of those who dare to claim His Name. Shame on us who sing of His cross on Sunday and crucify Him afresh all week!

### SEPTEMBER 11

### MAJORING ON THE MINOR

*These ought ye to have done, and not to leave the other undone.* MATTHEW 23:23.

JESUS WAS NOT preaching mainly on tithing here. Some have emphasized the negative side of this admonition until it has been overlooked that our Lord is pleading for "the weightier matters of the law, judgment, mercy and faith."

When Christians "major on the major," put first things first, and give proper attention to their faith in and fellowship with Christ, they will not leave lesser things undone. We are in peril of getting people to join church, tithe, and observe certain religious duties which, indeed, ought not to be left undone, but still omitting the supreme things which they should do first. Such procedure only confirms them in their self-righteousness and makes them doubly hard to reach with spiritual "first things." Don't forget that the Pharisees read the Scriptures, went to church, prayed, gave a tenth—and went to hell. Our righteousness must exceed theirs.

Let us "major on the major" and "minor on the minor."

## SEPTEMBER 12

### GOD'S COMPENSATIONS

*The Lord is able to give thee much more than this.*
II CHRONICLES 25:9.

AMAZIAH HAD HIRED an army of Israel to fight Edom, when he should have relied upon God. When a prophet advised against it Amaziah was concerned about the money he had paid out for such assistance. The prophet answered with our text. In other words, God is able to make up any loss we sustain when we give up anything for Him.

We are prone to seek help from the world when confronted with a crisis. To give it up leaves us with a helpless feeling. What about the sacrifices we make and the money we lose? But we only give up trash for treasures and rags for riches. God can and will abundantly compensate us for any loss we sustain. After all, we never lose anything by utter reliance on God. We but get rid of hindrances. It is never a losing proposition to trust God. When to us to live is Christ, then to die is gain, and even death pays dividends.

The Lord is able to give us much more than we lose when we part with all else to trust Him.

## SEPTEMBER 13

*I will even make a way in the wilderness.* ISAIAH 43:19.

WHEN I TREAD an unknown maze and can discern no path I find myself humming a little chorus:

"My Lord knows the way through the wilderness;
    All I have to do is to follow.
    Strength for the day,
    Is mine all the way,

And all that I need for tomorrow.
My Lord knows the way through the wilderness;
All I have to do is to follow."

"Thou knewest my path." "I being in the way the Lord
led me." "He leadeth me . . ." "Commit thy way . . ." Oh,
the Book is full of it—My Lord knows the way!

Better still, He *is* the way. It was an African guide who
said, "There is no way. . . . I am the way." My Lord offers
me no road map to figure out alone. He Himself is the Way,
and He goes along. That is so much better. I might get lost
on a path, I need a Person. He is my Way and . . .

"All I have to do is to follow."

### BY PARADISE AND THORN TO CHRIST

*Caught up into paradise . . . a thorn in the flesh. . . .*
*My grace is sufficient.* II CORINTHIANS 12:4, 7, 9.

PAUL'S PARADISE EXPERIENCE and the thorn given to offset
it lest he be exalted above measure—from height to depth—
were necessary to bring him to life's richest experience,
the daily sufficiency of Christ. We may need a crisis to
precipitate the matter, bring it to a head, but trips to the
third heaven and thorns in the flesh are incidental to life's
greatest lesson, to find in Christ Himself everything and
draw from Him His resurrection life for body, mind, and
spirit.

To stop short of that is to have an immature and inadequate experience. Occasional high days, answers to prayer
now and then, temporary blessings, make an uneven and
spasmodic Christian life. But to live day in and out, all
kinds of days, in simple dependence on Christ as the branch
on the vine, constantly abiding, that is the supreme experi-

ence. Not always glamorous and exciting but always sure, it is far better than an erratic, up-and-down, paradise-and-thorn existence. "A man in Christ"—that is it!

## SEPTEMBER 15

### GOD AND TITUS

*I found no rest in my spirit, because I found not Titus my brother. . . . Our flesh had no rest, but we were troubled on every side; without were fightings, within were fears. Nevertheless God, that comforteth those that are cast down, comforted us by the coming of Titus.* II CORINTHIANS 2:13; 7:5, 6.

THANK GOD FOR the humanness of Paul! Every lonely preacher, far from home, without rest in flesh or spirit, finds a kindred soul in these verses. We miss Titus, whether a brother or a dear one far from us. True, we have God, but we need the touch of a human hand and God often comforts us by Titus. It takes both God and Titus to cheer the cast-down. Paul had his helpers, like Onesiphorus, who oft refreshed him, and like Luke and Timothy.

But when the day came that "all men forsook" him, he could say, "Notwithstanding the Lord stood with me." There may come a time when Titus cannot reach us, but when it comes God will get through. And in the last valley where the dearest cannot go along we need fear no evil "for thou art with me."

## SEPTEMBER 16

### "TRUST ALSO . . ."

*Commit thy way unto the Lord; trust also in him; and he shall bring it to pass.* PSALM 37:5.

"ROLL THY WAY upon the Lord" is a marginal reading. Alas, we go through the form of it but fail to do the next thing, "trust also in him." We take our burden to the Lord, but we do not leave it there. We keep praying over the same ground, committing and recommitting our way. That is not faith, it is unbelief.

A man quietly reading a newspaper may not look as pious as a man on his knees in prayer. But if he has committed his way to the Lord and left it with Him, while he calmly moves on to something else, he is a better Christian than one who never leaves his way with the Lord but is always trying to. It looks very religious to keep on begging God to take over our burden, but true faith casts all care upon Him because He said to do it, and then considers it settled and stops worrying about it.

When Hannah brought her request to God, she considered it settled: "so the woman went her way and did eat and her countenance was no more sad." That is it! Go your way, eat and smile—it is as good as done when God takes over.


## SEPTEMBER 17

### SHOUTING AT JERICHO

*Shout; for the Lord hath given you the city.* JOSHUA 6:16.

THE PEOPLE SHOUTED *before* the walls fell. Anybody can shout after they fall. Faith anticipates victory and celebrates in advance.

"What things soever ye desire, when ye pray, believe that ye receive them, and ye shall have them" (Mk. 11:24). "Believe that ye receive them"—the walls are as good as down already when God says so. Faith takes His word for the deed and shouts now.

195

"The Lord hath given you the city." He has given us all things freely with the gift of His Son. We already have it in Christ, though we may not actually have possessed our possessions. Faith is the land deed for our inheritance with God's signature.

Jericho may loom big and ominous, but if, like Joshua, you have had a meeting with the Captain of the Lord's host, fear not. "Shout; for the Lord hath given you the city." Anticipate victory and shout in advance!

## SEPTEMBER 18

### "WE KNOW NOT . . . BUT THE SPIRIT"

*Likewise the Spirit also helpeth our infirmities.* RO-MANS 8:26.

"I CAN'T THINK or pray or feel as I ought. What shall I do?" You never will be able to do or be perfectly as you wish you might while you are in the flesh. You are a child of Adam, and the best falls far short. How often have we resolved, yielded, committed, dedicated ourselves, and then felt how poorly we had done it! No one ever prayed a prayer or preached a sermon that completely satisfied him. We are not to look in that direction for satisfaction.

Paul says in Romans 8 that we do not even know what to pray for as we ought, let alone how to pray, but the Spirit makes up our lack. God knows the intent of the heart, however poorly the lips express it.

If you can't pray like you want to, pray as you can. God knows what you mean. And you have good help—the Advocate who is God's Son and the Paraclete who is God's spirit. They will take your feeblest prayer and make it perfect.

196

## DON'T STOP AT A GRAVE!

*And Rachel died . . . and Israel journeyed.* GENESIS
35:19, 21.
*Moses my servant is dead; now therefore arise, go over
this Jordan.* JOSHUA 1:2.
*And his disciples came, and took up the body, and
buried it, and went and told Jesus.* MATTHEW 14:12.

JACOB BURIED HIS beloved Rachel—and journeyed on. When
Moses died Joshua took charge and crossed over Jordan.
John the Baptist died, and his disciples brought their grief
to Jesus.

No matter how deep your loss, how impossible it seems
to go on, life is too short to stop by any grave. We must
proceed. Loved ones pass away, great leaders die, the
prophet is beheaded. But God's work goes on and we must
go on. Those we have lost awhile would not have us settle
at their graves. God would have us arise and cross Jordan.

Bring your loss to Jesus, but do not sit up with the past.
For He said, "Let the dead bury their dead, *but go thou . . .*"

## SEPTEMBER 20

### WHEN THE CIRCUS DID NOT HINDER

*Having favour with all the people . . . but the people
magnified them.* ACTS 2:47; 5:13.

"IT WILL BE a bad week for our revival. We have the fair,
the concert, the circus, football this week. The Sons and
Daughters of I Will Arise have a supper, the high school
has a dance." On and on it goes, while defeated church
members build up their alibis. Any church that has to take
a back seat and fearfully anticipate every side show that
blows into town is already beaten. We have developed an
inferiority complex before the world, the flesh and the

devil, and apologetically we take what is left in attendance after our worldly members have gone where they really belong.

The Early Church did not quake every time the ungodly had a spree in Jerusalem. The saints in Rome did not have the blues because attendance would be cut by a gladiatorial contest in the Colosseum. They had a robust, world-shaking power of their own that eventually put the Colosseum out of business. If we recovered that we would leave our little hot-chocolate huddles in church basements and give the world today a demonstration that would make its little affairs look like firecrackers beside atom bombs.

## SEPTEMBER 21

### "SO LONG TIME—AND YET"

*Have I been so long time with you and yet hast thou not known me, Philip?* JOHN 14:9.

POOR, DULL, MATTER-OF-FACT Philip! Three years with Jesus, His preaching, His teaching, His miracles, Himself— *and yet!* "Shew us the Father and it sufficeth us." And for three years he had been looking right at the supreme revelation of the Father! "So long time—*and yet!*"

But we have no business feeling embarrassed and ashamed of Philip. For two thousand years we have had His presence, His church, the Spirit, the Word—and look at us! And some of us are well over life's hill and He has been with us all the way—*so long time and yet!* How poorly we know Him, how slow of heart to believe, how little like Him!

No, I will not blush for Philip, I will blush for myself. Is there a duller disciple anywhere? Forgive me, Lord. I need shed no tears for Philip, I should weep for myself.

"So long time . . . *and yet!*"

198

## SEPTEMBER 22

### VETERANS' RIGHTS

*Let not him that girdeth on his harness boast himself as
he that putteth it off.* I KINGS 20:11.

NOWADAYS, WHEN MOST churches want young pastors and
so much of our religious world is geared to youth, there is
still something to be said for the voice of age and experience. It bespeaks a dangerous modern mood that mature
and seasoned men find young Rehoboam disposed to scorn
their counsel for the rash advice of youngsters.

We have always needed old people to keep things from
going too fast and young people to keep them from going
too slow. Youth has fire and age has light and we need
both. "If only youth knew how and old age could!"

Some things come only with the passing of years, and
the fruit of wisdom cannot be produced by any hurried
process. Some things we must wait for. A mellowed Christian character cannot be grown hurriedly by any quick,
overnight method. Paul at the end of his course and the
finish of his fight has an advantage over Timothy. The old
soldier laying down his armor still has an earned veteran's
right over the most promising recruit.

### SEPTEMBER 23

### THE FIRST "PROSPECT"—YOURSELF!

*If my people . . . shall humble themselves . . .*
II CHRONICLES 7:14.
*If any man will come after me, let him deny himself.*
MATTHEW 16:24; MARK 8:34; LUKE 9:23.
*The churches of Macedonia . . . first gave their own
selves to the Lord.* II CORINTHIANS 8:1, 5.

DR. TORREY'S FIRST rule for revival was, "Let a few members of any church get thoroughly right with God them-

selves." Then they might go after others, but not until then. In their zeal for new members too many churches urge old members into visiting and canvassing "prospects," when first they need to get right with God themselves. We have no business going out to win others until we have faced our own condition first. Such activity may keep us from first giving ourselves to God. We may become occupied with others and thus dodge our own need. When Christians are right with God they will win others. Our revivals are stressing an "ingathering" of others, when God wants us to humble *ourselves*, deny *ourselves*, give *ourselves*. A drive for "prospects" before we do that is no revival at all.

## SEPTEMBER 24

### CHRIST'S PROGRAM FOR EPHESUS

*Remember therefore from whence thou art fallen, and repent, and do the first works.* REVELATION 2:5.

A REVIVAL IS *the church remembering, the church repenting, the church repeating.* Modern Ephesus may be orthodox and busy but she is far from her first love. She must have her mind stirred up by way of remembrance. She must discover how far she has slipped from her first estate. This is not easy and often is resented, for she may be very proud of her works and labor and patience and her hatred of the deeds of the Nicolaitanes. But revival begins with remembering, and to "jog the memory" is not easy for a preacher in Ephesus.

The church must *repent*, as our Lord commanded five out of seven churches in Asia to do. The average "revival" gets nowhere near a call to genuine repentance. And the church must *repeat*, do again the first works. To halt all the vast machinery today until we remember, repent, and repeat the first works would disrupt our program. So we dispense with real revival and face the "or else" of *removal*; "I will remove thy candlestick out of his place, *except thou repent.*"

### TARRYING AT BESOR

*As his part is that goeth down to the battle, so shall his part be that tarrieth by the stuff: they shall part alike.* I SAMUEL 30:24.

TWO HUNDRED OF David's men could not go on with him in the pursuit of the Amalekites. They were faint and stayed at the brook Besor. When the four hundred who went on returned with the spoils of victory, some did not want to share with those who had lingered behind. But, in the words of our text, David ruled otherwise.

For one reason or another, a lot of us do not get over Besor. We ought not to be faint, and all honor to the hardy souls who can "take it." But none of us has anything that he did not receive, and we show better spirit by sharing with weaker saints than in all our exploits against the enemy.

Some precious souls are housed in feeble bodies or otherwise kept at Besor. They never make the headlines with the front-line four hundred. But some prayed and toiled to keep hardier souls in the battle, and when the final prizes are awarded "they shall part alike."

### DO YOU NEED SOMETHING NEW?

*Behold, I will do a new thing.* ISAIAH 43:19.

SOMETIMES THE LADIES decide they need new hats or suits. They have gotten into a rut, they think, and something new would give them a lift. There is a psychological boost in a fresh outfit, as even the men know.

It is possible for Christians to become threadbare in experience. They run on past blessings and eat stale manna. Their testimonies begin to sound like well-worn phonograph records, sometimes cracked and a little scratchy.

We should not evermore be seeking some new "blessing," but we can get to where we look shiny when we ought to be shining. God likes to do a new thing for us. Many a church thinks it needs a new pastor when it needs the same pastor renewed. Many a restless saint needs not a new pasture where the grass always looks greener but a new thing done in his heart while he lives in the same pasture.

Let God do a new thing for you!

## SEPTEMBER 27

### "IF ANY MAN SIN"

*If any man sin . . .* I JOHN 2:1.
*If we confess our sins . . .* I JOHN 1:9.
*If we walk in the light . . .* I JOHN 1:7.

WE SHOULD NOT sin, but if we do sin we have an Advocate with the Father. We have a prosecutor, and an accuser, the devil; but we also have a lawyer to plead our case, Jesus Christ the righteous.

If we confess our sins the Father will forgive and cleanse. There must be genuine repentance and confession, but we need not wallow in remorse. God is our Father, if we believe and we are His children. And like as a father pitieth his children, so the Lord pitieth them that fear Him.

"If we walk in the light as he is in the light, we have fellowship one with another; and the blood of Jesus Christ his Son cleanseth us from all sin." Provision has been made for victory over sin. God's plan is to keep us from sin, not to keep us in sin. There is no ground for complacent living in iniquity just because we are "under the blood." "It is not that we are not able to sin but that we are able not to sin." But He also has made provision if we do sin, forgiveness and cleansing if we confess.

## SEPTEMBER 28

### THE SUPREME OBJECTIVE

*When thou wast young, thou girdest thyself, and walkedst whither thou wouldest: but when thou shalt be old, thou shalt stretch forth thy hands, and another shall gird thee, and carry thee whither thou wouldest not.* JOHN 21:18.

JESUS IS SPEAKING to Peter, and the explanation follows: "This spake he signifying by what death he should glorify God." What a picture, not only of impetuous, headstrong Peter but of us all in our early days when we did our own will and walked in our own way! We girded ourselves and walked where we wished and prided ourselves that we lived our own lives.

But the man who meets Jesus and submits to His sway comes to the day, blundering and stumbling as badly as Peter ever did, when he submits to what he does not choose for himself, even to death itself. And why? "This spake he signifying by what death he should glorify God." Our sole business, whether by life or by death, is just that, *to glorify God.* And when we discover that and do it, we have arrived.

## SEPTEMBER 29

### "PLEASURES FOREVERMORE"

*O the depth of the riches both of the wisdom and knowledge of God! How unsearchable are his judgments and his ways past finding out.* ROMANS 11:33.

PAUL IS OVERWHELMED by the magnitude of his theme. And well may any believer go into raptures over the treasure we have in Christ Jesus in whom dwells all the fulness of the Godhead bodily, by whom all things consist. Should there ever be a dull moment when every moment, any moment, affords time to know Him, the power of His resurrection and the fellowship of His sufferings? How can any preacher ever run out of sermons, with all this to ponder and preach? We shall be exploring the depths of it through all eternity. Shame on us that we take it for granted and get used to it here!

Here is a fountain that will never run dry, a treasure that can never be used up, a wealth that can never be exhausted. All other pursuits and quests and interests pale, but the riches of God in Christ Jesus will thrill us forever. Hallelujah!

## SEPTEMBER 30

### THE BEST IS YET TO BE

*So also is the resurrection of the dead. It is sown in corruption: it is raised in incorruption.* I CORINTHIANS 15:42.

ACHES AND PAINS remind us that the bodies we got from old Adam are disintegrating. Some of them look very unsightly before they are laid away, and often we are acutely aware that "it is sown in corruption." But the Christian anticipates a new body "like unto his glorious body" as part of his salvation. Everything we have by the first Adam is marred and spoiled and subject to decay. But when we become sons of God by faith in the last Adam we are assured a new body incorruptible, beyond the reach of sin, disease, and death. This removes the sense of futility such as torments the aging man without hope in Christ. The best

204

is yet to be! Lovely landscapes may wither, but a new earth looms ahead. Strong bodies may fail, but they only make way for new ones infinitely stronger. Loved ones go, but all who are in Christ are headed for a better reunion. "Christians never meet for the last time."

Cheer up, my brother! This body may never die, for Jesus may come first. But at worst it is only sown in corruption for an incorruptible harvest. We can't lose!

## OCTOBER 1

### TRUST AND TELL

*With the heart man believeth unto righteousness; and with the mouth confession is made unto salvation.*
ROMANS 10:10.

WE DO NOT have to pray a certain number of hours or weep a certain quantity of tears in order to be saved. Him that cometh to Jesus as best he knows how will in no wise be cast out. There are no exceptions. Faith is not a strenuous attitude of mind, a tense effort to believe. Faith is not merely refusing to doubt. The essence of saving faith is trust, stretching out relaxed on what God has said. We get our minds on ourselves, how well we stretch out, how much we relax, instead of on our support, the Word of God.

The insomniac cannot sleep, because he tries to hold up the bed. He cannot let go and let the bed hold him up. He may not be lying in a perfect position, but the bed holds him up just the same. Your faith may not be perfect, but God's promises are. You can never trust yourself, but you can always trust Christ. It is a heart-and-mouth experience. Trust Him and tell it!

## OCTOBER 2

### ABIDING AND ABOUNDING

*He that abideth in me and I in him, the same bringeth
forth much fruit.* JOHN 15:5.

WHY DO SO few Christians do business *for* God in daily public life? Because they do no business *with* Him in private
devotional life. When people do not mean business with
Christ in their hearts they will not do business for Christ
with their hands. Too often there has been mental acceptance of a proposition without heart surrender to a
Person. There has been a superficial profession: the Word
has been heard and even received with joy, but there has
been "no root." Or there has been a superficial dedication,
like the son in the parable, who said, "I go, sir," but did not
show up in the vineyard. If all who have "volunteered" to
be missionaries had gone the world would have been
evangelized.

When we really abide in Christ we bring forth much
fruit. Alas, many branches will be cast into the fire and
burned. If we are truly "with" Him we will gather for Him
(Mt. 12:30).

Those who mean business *with* Him do business *for* Him.
When we abide we abound.

### OCTOBER 3

### "I HAVE NO MAN . . ."

*Sir, I have no man, when the water is troubled, to put
me into the pool: but while I am coming, another
steppeth down before me.* JOHN 5:7.

THIS POOR MAN had been waiting for his chance to get into
the healing waters for a long, long time. Today a crippled

and infirm world crowds the pools of Bethesda. But how many never quite make it to healing and release! Whatever they seek, somebody else beats them to it.

In the presence of the Son of God this man was bemoaning the fact that he had no one to help him: "Sir, I have no man . . ." Are you waiting for human help to get you to your heart's desire? Better than all angel-troubled waters, better than the vain help of man, there stands One saying, "Wilt thou be made whole?"

Never were earth's pools of Bethesda as crowded as today. But you do not have to wait for an angel—some strange unearthly intervention—nor for a man—mere human assistance. Greater than angels or men, Jesus is at hand. Put your case in His hands and do His bidding. Men turn today to the supernatural in unguided mysticism and to the human in unspiritual psychiatry. All that you need is Jesus.

## OCTOBER 4

### BACK TO DOGMA!

*The time will come when they will not endure sound doctrine.* II TIMOTHY 4:3.

ONE OF THE pet bugaboos of many a deluded soul in the past few years has been dogma. One would think it the unpardonable sin to be dogmatic in the pulpit. Now we are reaping the harvest, because "my humble opinion" has supplanted "Thus saith the Lord."

When I am sick I want a dogmatic physician who knows what ails me and calls it by its right name. I want my medicine put up by a dogmatic pharmacist. If he got tired of being dogmatic and decided to disregard his formula it might mean my funeral. When I ride the train I want a dogmatic engineer up front who keeps a schedule. When your car needs repairs you want a dogmatic mechanic who knows what the trouble is and can fix it.

Yet in the pulpit, of all places, ministers to whom is entrusted the care of men's souls throw away their instructions and go by guesswork instead of by God's Word. We are not peddlers of fable. God has spoken, and when men ask a reason for our hope we ought to have a definite, clear-cut answer.

The Early Church did something because it believed something. We are trying to do what they did without believing what they believed. But without Scriptural doctrine we cannot do our spiritual duty.

## OCTOBER 5

### FIGS FROM THISTLES

*Either make the tree good, and his fruit good; or else make the tree corrupt, and his fruit corrupt: for the tree is known by his fruit.* MATTHEW 12:33.

WE URGE PEOPLE to join church, go to church, work in the church, tithe, sing in the choir, teach a class, and all too often the Lord is not adding such as are being saved—we are merely adding such as are being enlisted. We have corrupt trees endeavoring to produce good fruit. The church has recruited what God has not regenerated. The springs of their lives have not been reached, the source has not been dealt with. No wonder we coax and beg and entice by means diverse and often doubtful in order to persuade people to do what should be the spontaneous expression of their heart's love for Christ.

"Do men gather grapes of thorns, or figs of thistles?" We do not change the nature of our thorns by tying on the grapes of religious activity. We had better begin to aim at new creatures instead of just nice people. The intake may be smaller and statistics less impressive, but the fruit will be genuine.

## OCTOBER 6

### AN APPOINTMENT WITH GOD

*God . . . commandeth all men everywhere to repent:*
*because he hath appointed a day in the which he will*
*judge the world in righteousness by that man whom he*
*hath ordained.* ACTS 17:30, 31.

WE HAVE AN appointment with God. Many a man is careful to keep business and social engagements who ignores the supreme date on his calendar. God has set a day, He has ordained a judge, Christ Jesus. And this is the test by which men are judged, that light is come into the world in Jesus Christ and men loved darkness rather than light because their deeds were evil. By the Man He has ordained He will judge the world on the day appointed.

And because of this He has commanded repentance. He does not merely invite us to repent, He does not simply suggest that we repent, He *commands* it against the background of the Man Ordained and the Day Appointed. Too much preaching today lacks the solemn background of approaching judgment. It is politely recommended that men repent when God sternly commands it.

Men need to be reminded of their appointment with God, their date with Deity. The Day is appointed, the Man is ordained, and we are commanded. Put it on your calendar. It is on God's!

### OCTOBER 7

### GET THROUGH TO JESUS!

*If I may touch but his clothes, I shall be whole.* MARK
5:28.

IN THE MAZE of present-day confusion, the chaos of conflicting voices, how often have we wished that we might just

209

press through and touch Jesus as in the days of His flesh. They were not bewildered then by scholars and sectarians, each claiming the only perfect right to introduce anyone to Him. This poor sick woman came all by herself and for herself and it worked. Whether she had pure, unadulterated, unalloyed faith I know not, but she got through to Jesus!

Are you troubled and dizzy with a dozen voices shouting in your ears? Have you, like the father of the demonized boy, brought your problem to the disciples—this church or preacher—to find that "they could not"? Don't go away. Jesus is saying, "Bring your problem to me."

Push through the crowd and touch Him for yourself. You need no middleman to present you. As many as touch Him are made whole.

"Be whole of thy plague," He told the woman. Bring your plague to Him. Let no one stop you short of *Him.* "As many as touched *him* . . ."

### PUBLICIZING OUR PIETY

*Moreover, when ye fast, be not as the hypocrites, of a sad countenance: for they disfigure their faces, that they may appear unto men to fast. Verily I say unto you, They have their reward.* MATTHEW 6:16.

THERE IS NO holiness in a hair shirt or godliness in gunny-sack garments. "To be all out for God you don't have to look all in." The man who advertises his devotional life has not learned the most elementary rule of the devotional life —that it is a strictly private affair between him and his God.

Wearing cheap clothes if one can wear a good suit that will look better and last twice as long is false economy and not even good sense, let alone a mark of deeper holiness. God is not honored by penny-wise and pound-foolish living. We ought not to attract attention either by extravagance or negligence. A man may be trying to publicize his piety by faded garments, while he rails at the brother in fancy garb.

"Moses wist not that his face shone." The hypocrites were conscious of a sad face; Moses was unconscious of a shining face. Think it over.

## OCTOBER 9

### WE GAIN AS WE GIVE

*He which soweth sparingly shall reap also sparingly; and he which giveth bountifully shall reap also bountifully.* II CORINTHIANS 9:6.

GOD "GIVETH LIBERALLY." He is a generous God, and His children should never be misers. He loves a cheerful giver and "the liberal soul shall be made fat."

Mary used expensive ointment when she anointed Jesus, not a cut-rate bargain. It was Judas, who pilfered the treasury, who grumbled about Mary's generosity. God does not smile upon extravagance, but He does reward the bountiful sower. His servants are worthy of their hire, and Paul, though he sought nothing for himself, ever exhorted the saints to be liberal in their giving. When Christians turn into tightwads and try to do God's work as cheaply as possible they get cheap results. God will not honor a stingy testimony. The church that puts on a bargain revival cheats itself. God's work is in no danger of bankruptcy when His people are hilarious in their giving and hospitable to His servants.

God hates a false economy that is out to reduce a budget instead of to receive a blessing. We reap as we sow here, just as anywhere else.

## LIVING A DOUBLE LIFE

*They feared the Lord, and served their own Gods.*
II Kings 17:33.

The Lord was the God of their lips but not of their lives. And their number is legion today who give God the allegiance of lip but not life. Our Lord described them, quoting from Isaiah: "This people draweth nigh me with their mouth, and honoreth me with their lips; but their heart is far from me." He asked, "Why call ye me Lord, Lord, and do not the things which I say?" Paul writes of those "who profess that they know God; but in works they deny him."

It is an awful hypocrisy that declares with the lips what it denies with the life. We lie when we profess to fear the Lord at 11 A.M. on Sunday after we have served our own gods all week. "Thou shalt worship the Lord thy God and him only shalt thou serve." Worship and work must bear the same witness. It is what we serve that tells the tale. The shame of too many church members is that they lead a double life; they fear the Lord and serve their own gods.

## ROYAL ROBES AND SACKCLOTH

*And it came to pass, when the king heard the words of the woman, that he rent his clothes; and he passed by upon the wall and the people looked, and, behold, he had sackcloth within upon his flesh.* II Kings 6:30.

Jehoram, walking the walls of famine-stricken Samaria, wore a king's garments without but sackcloth next to his flesh. What a picture of this poor world today, spiritually starving, trying to be gay without to hide the gloom within! The robes of royalty without but the rags of a beggar within!

How it illustrates the plight of every sinner bedecked without in the colorful garb of this world but clad in the filthy rags of self-righteousness in his inmost soul!

Alas, there are too many in our churches robed in a profession of piety, a form of godliness; but beneath the sham, the shame—the sackcloth of fear and doubt and sin.

What a Samaria of hunger and want is ours today! God grant us a few lepers in the gate, as in the long ago, who will venture forward to find the bounty that God has prepared for all who trust Him and who refuse to sit still until they die!

### OCTOBER 12

### "ANY TIME" OR "GOD'S TIME"?

*Shew thyself to the world. . . . My time is not yet come: but your time is always ready.* JOHN 7:4, 6.

JESUS' UNBELIEVING BRETHREN thought He was not handling His publicity right. Why didn't He get out of the backwoods in Galilee and go up to Jerusalem, the capital, where He would be noticed and could demonstrate Himself?

How little they understood Jesus! God's ways are not ours. The church too often has followed the counsel of unbelievers and "shewed itself" to the world. God does not run His business after the pattern of this age.

"Your time is always ready," Jesus told His brethren. The man of this world is always in season, for this is the season of this world. But when the world passes and the lusts thereof, the man who does God's will abides forever.

He who walks in God's way has a schedule and must await God's time for this and that. But for the unbeliever "one time is as good as another." The world knows nothing of seeking the mind of the Lord before doing this or that. But those who acknowledge Him in all their ways find that He directs their paths.

213

## OCTOBER 13

### BLINDED BY "SEEING"

*For judgment I am come into this world, that they which see not might see; and that they which see might be made blind.* JOHN 9:39.

THIS TERRIFYING PRONOUNCEMENT ought to jolt some complacent souls today. It grows out of that dramatic incident in which the Pharisees, religious, separated, praying Bible scholars, called Jesus a *sinner*, while a poor blind man, just healed, eagerly and immediately believed on Him as the *Son of God*. The application does not end in John. Churchmen, deacons, trustees, even ministers, who say, "We see," have failed to know Jesus when He passed by in the day of their visitation, while some poor sinner who knew no theology has gladly cried, "I believe." The possibilities in the meaning of this verse are alarming and could cause consternation in some well-ordered church on Sunday morning were some man of the street to get saved to the disgust, maybe, of a chief elder.

Beware that you are not blinded by your "sight," saying, "I see," while "your sin remaineth."

## OCTOBER 14

### "ALL TO HIM I OWE"

*Ye are bought with a price.* I CORINTHIANS 6:20.

WE ARE NOT our own, we have been redeemed. But while we sing "Jesus Paid It All" let us remember the next line, "All To Him I Owe." Certain Divine requirements grow out of our being bought with a price. Such love demands my soul, my life, my all. We are to glorify God in body and spirit—our *selves*—because we belong to Him (I Cor. 6:19, 20). We are to glorify Him in our *service:* "Ye are bought

214

with a price; be not ye the servants of men" (I Cor. 7:23). And Peter tells us that since we have been redeemed with the precious blood of Christ, we are to pass the time of our *sojourning* here in fear (I Pt. 1:17–21).

*Self, service, sojourning*—all to Him I owe, because He paid it all. While we sing about the price that He paid, we had better check on what God expects for us, not to repay Him, but as the expression of our heart's love to Him who redeemed us.


## OCTOBER 15

### MORNING AFTER

*But when the morning was now come, Jesus stood on the shore: but the disciples knew not that it was Jesus.*
JOHN 21:4.

AFTER A NIGHT of fruitless fishing—it had happened before (Lk. 5:5)—the disciples did not recognize the risen Lord upon the shore. How much of our labor is in vain because it is our own poor little expedition (see verse 3)! But our labor is not in vain when it is in the Lord.

There is a beautiful progression in this story. John recognizes the stranger. "It is the Lord!" Peter immediately leaps into the water and heads for shore. He has denied his Lord and had been out of fellowship, but when he heard Jesus was on the shore, he went toward Him, not from Him.

Jesus invited them to a prepared meal, and they knew it was the Lord. He becomes real to all who accept His invitation and take what He offers.

Has it been a fisherman's failure with you? Has your little venture come to nought? See the Lord upon the shore. Heed His instruction, and a night of defeat will give way to a morning of delight.

215

## LET GO AND LET GOD

*Cast thy burden upon the Lord, and he shall sustain thee.* PSALM 55:22.

SOME DEAR SOULS get the impression that faith is an attitude, a spiritual pose, which must be strenuously maintained for dear life. So they grit their teeth and screw themselves up to believe in tense earnestness, afraid to let go for a moment. We might as well try to pull ourselves up by our own bootstraps.

Trusting God is exactly the very opposite of all that. Hudson Taylor worked hard trying to develop faith, until he stopped looking at his faith and learned to rest in the Faithful one. You will blow up trying to work yourself up to just the right pitch. Faith begins by letting go, stretching out on the promises, not by taking a deep breath, clenching your fists, and resolving to trust or bust.

If we are to roll our burden upon the Lord, the only move on our part is to roll it, then leave it. Of course, if we never leave it, it rolls back and we spend all our time rolling instead of resting. He will keep what we commit—and leave committed.

"Let go and let God" is too often a proverb instead of a practice.

## "YET BELIEVING"

*Whom having not seen ye love; in whom, though now ye see him not,* yet believing, *ye rejoice with joy unspeakable and full of glory.* I PETER 1:8.

PETER HAD SEEN Jesus. His readers had not but they believed, anyway. Did not our Lord say a similar thing to

Thomas: "Thomas, because thou hast seen me, thou hast believed: blessed are they that have not seen *and yet have believed*"? (Jno. 20:29.)

It is not every man's privilege to see, but it is every man's privilege to believe. Our love and our faith do not rest upon sight. Neither does our rejoicing. We have "joy and peace *in believing* (Rom. 15:13).

Do not demand a vision. Only three saw the glory on the transfiguration mount. But all the disciples walked with our Lord in the valley. The others were not disqualified by missing the vision. It is not lack of sight but lack of faith that rules us out. "We walk by faith, not by sight" (II Cor. 5:7). *Yet believing*—anyhow!


## OCTOBER 18

### SECOND FIDDLE

*And now, behold, the king walketh before you: and I am old and grayheaded.* I SAMUEL 12:2.

SAMUEL WAS A better man than Saul, but he knew how to take a back seat graciously. Blessed are the Saints of the Second Fiddle! Some want to do solo work or be the whole orchestra. Saul had no grace for second place. When he heard the women singing, "Saul hath slain his thousands and David his ten thousands," he "was very wroth and the saying displeased him." Some preachers have been known to react that way when eclipsed by one more successful.

The best men are not always kings. "I have seen servants upon horses and princes walking as servants upon the earth." Diotrephes loves the pre-eminence. "In honor preferring one another"—surely that grace languishes for want of exercise!

John the Baptist was in his heyday as the foremost prophet and preacher of his time when he said of Jesus, "He must increase but I must decrease." God grant us the Beatitude of the Background, that only He may be seen!

Samuel took the back seat for a lesser, John the Baptist for a greater. Can you play second fiddle, whether for a lesser or for the Greatest of All?

## OCTOBER 19

### SIDE TRIP TO EGYPT

*Woe to them that go down to Egypt for help.*
ISAIAH 31:1.

ABRAM DID IT and got into an embarrassing predicament, denied his wife, and was sent out of the land. What a testimony for the Father of the Faithful! But he was not the only good man who visited Egypt in time of famine. We forget so easily that God can furnish tables in the wilderness. When times are hard we turn to the world for help. And sometimes Egypt offers a bigger salary!

We never need to leave Canaan and go back over Jordan for any reason whatsoever. We commonly think of the Promised Land as flowing with milk and honey, flourishing with figs and pomegranates. But sometimes God sends a drought and the pickings are slim and the garlic and onions and fleshpots tantalize us, tempt us to Egypt.

Are you passing through a dry spell and a lean season? Christians and churches are apt to turn to Pharaoh in spiritual famine. But it always means denial and embarrassment and humiliation and loss of testimony. All that we need we have in Canaan. No side trips are necessary. Settle down in Beulah Land and enjoy the country!

## OCTOBER 20

### WAITING FOR A KINGDOM

*A good man . . . who also himself waited for the king-
dom of God.* LUKE 23:50, 51.

SOME OF US are looking for a better day. We are waiting
for that time when God's kingdom shall come, when His
will shall be done on earth as in heaven. We seek a country.
We are strangers and pilgrims on this earth. We are not at
home here. Our citizenship is in heaven.

I know it looks to some as though the Kingdom were
nowhere near. It must have been a dark day for Joseph of
Arimathea when he laid away the body of Jesus. It looked
like the devil had everything going his way. But far from
it! Redemption's work had been finished, and the resurrection was only a few hours away!

Throughout this wretched world more hearts are waiting
for the Kingdom than we imagine. All other kingdoms are
coming to an end. More than one patient Joseph of Arimathea is humbly carrying on. Lift up your heads, all ye
who desire a better country. When things look darkest to
the world, they look brightest to the Christian. Our King is
coming back!

What better thing could be said of any mortal than this:
"A good man . . . who also himself waited for the kingdom
of God"?

## OCTOBER 21

### THE ULTIMATE VINDICATION

*That at the name of Jesus every knee should bow, of
things in heaven and things in earth, and things under
the earth; and that every tongue should confess that
Jesus Christ is Lord, to the glory of God the Father.*
PHILIPPIANS 2:10, 11.

THE PREACHER OF Christ, however much men may dis
agree with and oppose him now, has always the certainty

219

that one day everybody will agree with him. Some day every tongue will make it unanimous that Jesus is Lord. It will be too late for the salvation of most of them, but our Lord will receive universal homage.

That day will vindicate our faith in Him in the eyes of all creation. We can afford to wait for that, but no unbeliever can afford to wait.

The Lordship of Christ is the center of our faith. The believer's confession is, "Jesus is Lord." One day the universe will make it final: "Jesus is Lord." It is never a question of "Will you confess Him as Lord?" but "When?" Now, while you may be saved, or then, will it be too late?

Do not wait for that Ultimate Vindication. "If thou shalt confess with thy mouth Jesus as Lord and shalt believe in thine heart that God hath raised him from the dead, thou shalt be saved."

## OCTOBER 22

### NOT FAVORITES BUT INTIMATES

*Of a truth I perceive that God is no respecter of persons.*
Acts 10:34.
*And the Lord spake unto Moses face to face as a man speaketh unto his friend.* Exodus 33:11. . .

SOMEONE SAID IT well, "God has intimates but no favorites." He has no pets. He may seem to grant to some more success, greater blessings, than to others but, whatever the reasons are, known best to Himself, favoritism is not one of them. He sends rain upon the just and the unjust. He is no respecter of persons.

But He has closer fellowship with some, reveals Himself to them more fully, confides in them His deepest secrets. So He did with Enoch, with Abraham, "the friend of God," with Moses, not because of special merit in them or favoritism with Him, but because in His sovereign will He chose to do so.

Yet any man can know God more intimately. "Draw nigh to God and He will draw nigh to you." Jesus promised to manifest Himself to the obedient heart (Jno. 14:21). We are not servants but friends, and we can be close friends.

Do not expect to be a favorite, but aspire to be an intimate of God's. His secret is with them that fear Him.

## OCTOBER 23

### IF YOU CAN'T SEE, LOOK!

*Looking unto Jesus.* HEBREWS 12:2

WE ARE LOOKING unto Jesus, not at Him. There is a world of difference. F. B. Meyer says something to the effect that if we cannot see Him we can look in the direction where we know Him to be. Alexander Whyte puts it: "He does not say, See; He says only, Look"

The snake-bitten Israelite, far to the rear in the multitude, may not have been able to make out clearly the outline of the serpent, but he looked that way. What matters most is not how clearly we perceive Jesus but the utter dependence of our look. If a friend should assume a debt for us, we would look, not at him, but unto him, to meet the obligation. Sometimes our view grows dim and we cannot feel or think with satisfaction. Darkness veils Jesus' lovely face, but if we rest on His unchanging grace, looking His way in the fog, that is it.

Look His way, face His direction, as you move through the mist. Look unto Him, even though you cannot look at Him. He will not fail, though you cannot feel. He abideth faithful.

221

## ANGELS AHEAD

*And they said among themselves, Who shall roll us away the stone from the door of the sepulchre? And when they looked, they saw that the stone was rolled away: for it was very great.* MARK 16:3, 4.

OTHERS, LIKE DR. JOWETT, have caught the precious lesson of these verses. How often have we set out expecting trouble and dreading the difficulty ahead, to find upon arrival that God had "rolled away the stone"! Like the lepers in Samaria's gate, we venture forward, to find that God has scattered the enemy.

What "stone" lies ahead of you? You are wondering how you will get it rolled away, you lie awake all night making plans to remove tomorrow's obstacle. And how often have you reached the place appointed, to find that God had anticipated your dilemma.

Some stones we can roll away. "Take ye away the stone," commanded Jesus at Lazarus' grave. Some hindrances we can remove, and we must if the miracle is to follow. But the stone that is too big for us God's angel can handle.

Some saints in weakened condition wonder how it will be when they come to death. Fear not. The grave could not hold Jesus nor will it hold you. For Him the stone which enemies thought they had made sure would hold Him in the grave was turned into a throne of triumph with an angel sitting on it.

Do not walk in dread. God's angel will arrive at the dilemma first. Are you looking for stones ahead or angels ahead?

## THE CROWD OR THE CHRIST?

*And every man went unto his own house. [But] Jesus went unto the mount of Olives.* JOHN 7:53; 8:1.

OUR LONELY LORD, beset by the Pharisees, despised and rejected of men, took to the solitude of the Mount of Olives, while men returned to the comfort of their homes. He had nowhere to lay His head, having come to His own, who received Him not. Many a night He spent in prayer, while even His disciples slumbered.

This world still goes "every man to his own house." Alas, even we Christians do, for "all seek their own, not the things which are Jesus Christ's." We pursue our own interests, we live our own lives, we know nothing of the Mount of Olives' concern for the plight of our hearts, the condition of the church, the state of the world. We pay God our respects on Sunday, but we return to putter around our own premises. We sing, "I'll Go With Him Through The Garden," when the olive trees would never recognize us, for we never accompany our Lord there.

Our Lord was a solitary figure in His day, and to this hour the deeper Christian life is a lonely life. You will never "follow the crowd" to the Mount of Olives, for few go that way.

You can follow the crowd or the Christ, but not both, for they go in opposite directions.

## THE GREAT DIVIDER

*So there was a division among the people on account of him.* JOHN 7:43.

TWICE AGAIN JOHN tells us of division because of Jesus (9:16; 10:19). A lot of pleasant talk about unity these days forgets that Christ is the Great Divider. He came not to send peace but a sword, and expressly declared that He would divide families, so that a man's foes would be they of his own household (Mt. 10:34–36). He divides hearts, homes, churches, humanity. No man can take a stand for Christ without a cleavage. If we gather not with Him we scatter abroad.

But not all division is on account of Christ. "Mark them which cause divisions . . . and avoid them" (Rom. 16:17). There are trouble-makers who delight in schisms. Be sure your division is on account of Him, not "them."

But be not deceived by sweet talk about harmony that does not make Christ the issue. He is a sanctuary or a snare (Isa. 8:14) and there is no middle ground. Men fall on that Rock and are broken in repentance or that Rock falls upon them and breaks them in judgment.

He is the Great Divider, and He does not divide men horizontally—high class, middle class, low class—but vertically, to the right and to the left.

## OCTOBER 27

### GIVE GOD THE MACEDONIAN

*The churches of Macedonia . . . first gave their own selves to the Lord.* II CORINTHIANS 8:1, 5.

WE HAVE MONEY in the church today but not many Macedonians. People give their substance but not their selves. Fine churches are built, workers are employed, and the members show up on Sunday morning, but never dream of living for God seven days a week. Actually, every Christian is meant to be in full-time Christian service, whether he draws a salary for it or not. Jesus paid it all and all to Him we owe.

Silver and gold we have aplenty, but we are not saying

224

to a crippled world, "Rise and walk." Expensive edifices
built with "vain oblations"—gifts without the givers—cannot substitute for giving God the temples of our bodies and
hearts. Modern Macedonians give money, but the early
Macedonians first gave God the Macedonians! The Early
Church was all lay witnesses. Too often now it is big business run by a salaried staff paid to do church work, while
the rest of us work for ourselves. But we are all on the
staff, and no matter how faithfully salaried helpers may
work, they cannot do our job nor can we do ours merely
by paying them. God wants the Macedonian first.

## OCTOBER 28

### LOST AND FOUND

*He that findeth his life shall lose it: and he that loseth*
*his life for my sake shall find it.* MATTHEW 10:39.

MOST OF US are out to succeed, to achieve our own ends,
to accomplish our own goals and aims. But God operates
a Lost and Found Department, wherein a man loses himself
in Another, exchanges self-realization for Christ-realization.
It takes out all the fever and strain, the mad drive to reach
some goal this crazy world has set, or some mark we have
put up for ourselves. Today millions crack up in this insane
scramble, but the man who lives for Christ's sake finds by
losing what others lose forever trying to find.

You will observe that Jesus said, "He that loseth his life
*for my sake.*" Never forget that qualification. That rules out
mere altruism and idealism. Martyrs in scientific research,
men who lose themselves in music or art or medicine, soldiers on battlefields, do not necessarily come into this category. We must lose ourselves for His sake. Not even for
religion's sake—for His sake. We are inclined to take in
too much territory here.

God's "Lost and Found" operates "for Christ's sake."

## OCTOBER 29

### MAKE DISCIPLES

*Go ye therefore, and make disciples of all the na-
tions . . .* MATTHEW 28:17 (A.S.V.).

WE WOULD NOT strain for a point here, but it is evident that
we are to make disciples, not just believers. Of course, in
the Early Church there were no distinctions; a believer was
also a disciple and a witness. There was no taking Christ as
Saviour now, as Lord later—maybe never. Men confessed
with their mouths Jesus as Lord while they believed in their
hearts.

But today churches are filled with "believers" who have
never been made disciples. Some of them perform per-
functory religious duties, but they have never denied self,
taken up the cross, and followed Christ. They have not been
taught *to observe* all things commanded.

The early Christians believed, became disciples, and that
sent them out as witnesses to make disciples of others.

We need to learn our Great Commission all over again.


## OCTOBER 30

### THE DEPARTING ANGEL

*And forthwith the angel departed from him.* ACTS
12:10.

THE ANGEL HAD brought Peter out of prison through the
gate and safely outside. Now the miracle was over and the
angel took his leave. Peter was on his own.

God intervenes by His angel many a time to loose our
souls from prison. He does the supernatural thing when the
occasion demands it. But He does not perform miracles
when we can get along without them. He lets us do the

thing we can do for ourselves, all within the circles of His grace of course.

Peter shifted for himself when be came to and realized he was not dreaming. Some saints expect angels to wake them up and serve them breakfast in bed. Do not expect the supernatural when God would have you proceed in the normal natural course of things. Peter did not sit down and wait for another angel—he headed toward a prayer meeting.

Thank God for His angels, but they depart. Trust His indwelling Spirit to guide you every day, miracle or no miracle. Angels come and go, but He abides.

## OCTOBER 31

### HOW TO BE INDEPENDENT

*I have learned, in whatsoever state I am, therewith to be content.* PHILIPPIANS 4:11.

"CONTENT" HAS BEEN rendered "independent." Paul has learned in any state to be self-sufficient, independent, not in the haughty worldly sense but in that he lives by inner resources. He can do all things through Christ. While he deeply appreciates and rejoices in the love-gift sent to him by the Philippian saints, his sufficiency is not in the Lord's people but in God, who is able to supply every need.

The servant of the Lord who is looking to the Lord's people instead of unto the Lord will be nervous and sometimes disappointed. But the man who is looking unto Jesus about his finances as well as everything else will not worry whether his remuneration be a Philippian love-gift or a puny stipend. Not all churches may be as generous as the Philippians, but God's riches in glory by Christ Jesus are as abundant as in Paul's day.

Let us be independent of men, dependent on God.

227

## NOVEMBER 1

### CRISIS AND CONTINUANCE

*And they were all filled with the Holy Ghost. And they continued stedfastly.* ACTS 2:2, 42.

THE SAME CHAPTER records both Crisis and Continuance. Some of us major on one, some on the other. We need a synthesis of both. Ecstasies, high days, lofty experiences-- some go in for these but cannot maintain such a high-strung pitch and often run into excesses. Others major on the daily walk and growth in grace but tend to get into a rut.

Why not "a sea of glass mingled with fire," a combination of both Crisis and Continuance? "Tasks in hours of *insight* willed can be in hours of *gloom* fulfilled." "After he had seen the vision, immediately we endeavoured to go" (Acts 16:10). The Vision and the Venture!

The best evidence of being truly filled with the Spirit is that one so filled "continues daily." The Glory shows up in the Grind! As important as the Grandeur of Getting Started is the Grace of Going On!

## NOVEMBER 2

### REVIVE US AGAIN—BUT NOT NOW!

*Bring forth therefore fruits meet for repentance.* MATTHEW 3:8.

JOHN THE BAPTIST demanded real evidence of a change of heart. We live in an "epidemic" of so-called revivals the year round, but most church members weather them without repentance or the fruits thereof, renunciation and restitution. Most revivals begin with two or three sermons to the church and pass quickly into a drive for "prospects" and new church members, leaving the church quite unscathed.

We need a new John the Baptist putting the ax to the root, not the fruit, of the tree; calling for conviction-born repentance among Christians, a change of mind, godly sorrow, and confession and renunciation of sin, for he that "confesseth *and forsaketh* them shall have mercy"; and for restitution wherever possible—a straightening out of old accounts such as Zacchæus made.

This is revival—not just singing, "Revive Us Again," with no intention whatever of paying the price now!

## NOVEMBER 3

### WILLING AND WORKING

*Work out your own salvation with fear and trembling. For it is God which worketh in you both to will and to do of his good pleasure.* PHILIPPIANS 2:12, 13.

THIS COMBINATION MAKES it all the work of God and yet puts us to work. He does the willing and the working. But we "work out what He works in."

It is a blessed thing to know and to remind ourselves as we move through each day, "God is working in me to will and do of his good pleasure." But let us remember the other side of it: "I do always those things that please him" (Jno. 8:29). How few Christians ever think of working out their salvation *with fear and trembling* in these days of cheap and easy religion! A deep and sober daily concern to please God is the rarest of rarities.

God wills and works, but He moves us to will and work. Our feeble purpose and performance take on real importance when we realize that God is energizing both. The Father hath not left us alone. Therefore we are enabled by Him to do those things that please Him.

229

NOVEMBER 4

## "HE STAGGERED NOT"

*He staggered not at the promise of God through unbelief.* ROMANS 4:20.

FAITH DOES NOT nervously go over the same committal again and again. Faith goes on from there ruggedly believing that what God has promised He will perform. Abraham did not even consider what were really impossibilities. He considered God, not circumstances. So did Hannah when "she went her way and her countenance was no more sad." So did Paul in the storm at sea, when he said, "I believe God."

It is a mark of unbelief, not of faith, when we uneasily look around us and keep reminding God that we are depending on Him. We are trusting Him more when, instead of constantly reminding Him, we move on to do the next thing and the next, counting it all as good as done. A father would be grieved if his child kept on asking, "Are you sure you will take care of me?" A trusting child goes on about other things and wastes no time trying to trust its father.

You are not really trusting until you quit trying. The more you examine your faith, the sicklier it will be. Don't look at your faith. Look unto Jesus!

## NOVEMBER 5

### DON'T SETTLE HERE!

*Demas hath forsaken me, having loved this present world.* II TIMOTHY 4:10.

DEMAS HAD TO forsake something, for no man could follow Paul and the world at the same time. Paul was a stranger and a pilgrim, and "he sought a country." He had not

230

driven his tent pegs down in these lowlands of earth, nor had he hung his stocking for the Santa Claus of this age to fill. All who follow him as He follows Christ make this present world "their passage and not their portion, as Matthew Henry puts it.

The angels from their place on high
Look down on us with wondering eye,
That where we are but passing guests
We build such firm and solid nests;
But where we hope to live for aye
We scarce take heed one stone to lay.

Don't feather your nest down here. The path of the Word and the path of the world do not run parallel. You must forsake one to follow the other.

## NOVEMBER 6

### GOD BREAKS THROUGH!

*Since the fathers fell asleep, all things continue as they were from the beginning of the creation.* II PETER 3:4.

IT IS THE argument of the scoffers concerning the Lord's return, but it is used in a far wider range: "God is not interested in what becomes of us. God has not spoken with finality in the Bible. God did not take human form in Jesus Christ. Jesus was not virgin-born. He did not rise from the dead. He is not coming again. Men are born to be what they become, and there is no new birth. God does not guide and keep people. He does not answer prayer." In support of all this is the old argument: " 'All things continue as from the beginning of creation'; things run a natural course fixed by law, and God never breaks through."

231

But He has broken through in His Word and in His Son, and He does save and guide and keep and answer prayer. There is a higher law, not contra-natural, but supernatural.

No, things do not continue as they were from the beginning. God breaks through! How we need a fresh visitation! "Oh that thou wouldst rend the heavens . . . [and] come down!"

## NOVEMBER 7

### THE STAYED MIND

*Thou wilt keep him in perfect peace, whose mind is stayed on thee: because he trusteth in thee.* ISAIAH 26:3.

WE HAVE MASTERED many diseases of the body. Some of the worst plagues have been conquered and others may be on the way out. But now we are going crazy by the thousands and the mental hospitals are crowded. The devil is majoring on the mind. Too often mental sufferers are advised to lay up their Bibles, give religion a rest, and go to the movies.

Is the Lord not able to help us when we need Him most? If He can save and keep the soul, is it the best we can do to turn body and mind over to the wisdom of man? Is there no balm in Gilead for us here and now and grace to help in every time of need?

The average unstrung individual will find his inhibitions, complexes, neuroses, and other ailments straightened out by getting right with God and man. The stayed mind is a sound mind and belongs to him who trusts in God. Such a man is kept in perfect peace, not by tensely maintaining a certain mental attitude, God keeps him. And he lets God do it! "He careth for you." Then let Him!

232

*For the eyes of the Lord run to and fro throughout the whole earth, to shew himself strong in the behalf of them whose heart is perfect toward him.* II CHRONICLES 16:9.

GOD IS NOT waiting to show us strong in His behalf but Himself strong in our behalf. That makes a lot of difference. He is not out to demonstrate what we can do but what *He* can do. But God *is* on the lookout for candidates with hearts perfect toward Him. He is not a talent scout looking for somebody strong enough or good enough. He is looking for someone with a heart set on pleasing Him and an eye single to His glory. He will do the rest.

What a wonder that God will use our lives to demonstrate Himself! But we like to demonstrate ourselves and do great exploits in God's behalf. That reverses the process and God does not get the glory. We have seen enough of what men can do for God; we need to see more of what God can do through men.

He has shown Himself strong in our behalf many a time. And what He has done for others, He will do for you.

### "PROVE ME NOW"

*Call unto me, and I will answer thee, and shew thee great and mighty things, which thou knowest not.* JEREMIAH 33:3.

WE ARE INCLINED to pray as though this world were in the grip of cold, fixed laws, with only the remote possibility that God might occasionally break through. We timidly whisper a few feeble petitions barely *hoping*, but certainly not *believing* that we shall receive. But God is not a prisoner in His own universe. Jesus is the Lord of all creation, King of kings and Lord of lords. The devil can go only so far as God allows him to go.

God is waiting to show Himself strong in behalf of those whose heart is perfect toward Him. He invites us to prove Him. He longs to demonstrate what He can do, exceeding abundantly above all we ask or think, great and mighty things which we know not.

"Let us therefore come boldly unto the throne of grace, that we may obtain mercy and find grace to help in time of need."

This is our Father's world. God is still on the throne of creation. Call on Him and He will answer.

## NOVEMBER 10

### "THE CENTRAL VERITY"

*Wherefore I give you to understand, that no man speaking by the Spirit of God calleth Jesus accursed: and that no man can say that Jesus is the Lord, but by the Holy Ghost.* I CORINTHIANS 12:3.

DR. G. CAMPBELL MORGAN says Paul is here stating the central verity of the church, the absolute Lordship of Christ. Both the cult of Cæsar and the cult of Christ used the term *Kurios*. It was "Nero Kurios" (Nero Lord) or "Kurios Iesous" (Lord Jesus)—"the battle cries of the spirit of error and the spirit of truth." Polycarp the martyr paid with his life because he refused to call Cæsar, Lord, and said each time, "Lord Jesus."

Of course, it is easy to call Him, Lord, Lord, and not do His commands (Mt. 7:21–23). Only the Spirit of God can make real to the soul the Lordship of Jesus Christ. Just because Nero is dead makes no difference—there is still the cult of Cæsar, and a man cannot have two Lords. A day of cheap discipleship, with churches filled by baptized pagans, needs to be startled into taking seriously the battle cry, "Jesus Is Lord."

There are too many religious Sauls who need to become regenerated Pauls asking, "*Lord,* what wilt thou have me to do?"

## NOVEMBER 11

### BED-RIDDEN TRUTH

*If ye know these things, happy are ye if ye do them.*
JOHN 13:17.

OUR LORD CONDITIONS true happiness not on knowledge alone but on knowledge of His Word plus obedience.

Coleridge says: "Truths, of all others the most awful and interesting, are too often considered as *so* true that they lose the power of truth, and lie bed-ridden in the dormitory of the soul, side by side with the most despised and exploded errors."

Here lies a fearful peril to us all, that we take for granted the very things God never meant should become a matter of course, and because we know them so well and have heard them so often we assume that what is a fact in our heads is a force in our hearts. May it not be that this is why we never finish the verse, "Be ye doers of the word and not hearers only" by adding the most terrific part of it, *deceiving your own selves?* We pleasantly assent to a Gospel we ought powerfully to assert. How it needs to be rescued "from the neglect caused by the very circumstance of its universal admission"!

What great truth lies bed-ridden in the dormitory of your soul?

235

## THE TOUCHSTONE OF FAITH

*If thou shalt confess with thy mouth Jesus as Lord, and
shalt believe in thine heart that God hath raised him
from the dead, thou shalt be saved.* ROMANS 10:9
(A.S.V.).

HERE IS THE key to the sad state of many a Christian and
many a church today. There has been a cheap easy profession of Christ as Saviour but no real confession of Christ as
Lord. The lips claim Him as Saviour but the life shows no
evidence of His Lordship. We love the same things we have
always loved; we do not abhor that which is evil, we live
our own lives, Christ has no say in the matter.

A. T. Robertson said, "No Jew would do this who had not
really trusted Christ, for *Kurios* in the LXX [Septuagint] is
used of God. No Gentile would do it who had not ceased
worshiping the Emperor as *Kurios*. The word *Kurios* was
and is *the Touchstone of faith*."

It meant everything in those days to say, "Jesus is Lord."
There is one absolute test: Is Jesus Christ the Lord of your
life? Or are you "fearing the Lord and serving your own
gods"?

When our "believers" became real "disciples," then they
will be "witnesses." You cannot willingly take Jesus as
Saviour and wilfully deny Him as Lord. "Believe on the
*Lord* Jesus Christ, and thou shalt be saved."

### THE INTERCHANGEABLE TRIAD

*I in them, and thou in me* . . . JOHN 17:23.
*We are in him* . . . I JOHN 5:20.

GOD IS IN Christ, Christ is in us who believe, we are in
Christ—glorious identification that overflows all our figures

to describe it! The Head and the Body, the Vine and the Branches—we are partakers of the Divine Nature.

Our poor little word images cannot say it. Sometimes we try with illustrations from daily life. The iron is in the fire, we say; then the iron grows red and we say the fire is in the iron. But all such efforts fall short.

"Your life is hid with Christ in God"—that is one way of looking at it. Those two precious words, "In Christ," lie scattered like jewels all over the New Testament. "Christ liveth in me," "Christ in you the hope of glory"—that is another facet of this gem. And what a red-letter day it has been for many a soul when "Christ liveth in me" gets translated from theology into reality!

Anyway you look at it, this Interchangeable Triad is something to shout about. "Thou in me, I in them, we . . . in him."

### NOVEMBER 14

#### A LESSON IN ADDITION

*And the same day there were added unto them about three thousand souls. ACTS 2:41.*

FOR A CHURCH of three thousand members to take in one hundred and twenty more would be almost phenomenal these days. But here a fellowship of one hundred and twenty was suddenly augmented by three thousand. What a revival if that rate of increase were maintained!

How was it done? Through the preaching of Jesus Christ in the power of the Holy Spirit. There are additions and additions today, but how much of them is the Lord adding daily such as should be saved?

There is addition from without, like barnacles on a boat. There is addition from within, like grapes on a vine. It is to be feared that the church has encumbered herself with a

237

lot of excess baggage, not members of the body of Christ, but names in an organization.

You will observe that the Lord did the adding. He uses His appointed means, but He must do it if it is to be the genuine fruit of Pentecost.

Have you been added from without or from within?

## NOVEMBER 15

### KEEP STEP WITH GOD

*Enoch walked with God.* GENESIS 5:24.

ENOCH DID NOT run ahead of God or lag behind Him. He walked with Him. Some go too fast, they hasten to an immature and superficial experience with God, and their consecration is not thorough. They make a mechanical "decision," but the depths have never been stirred. Or else in a spell of emotion they make a hurried covenant with God but have no root or depth.

Others go too slowly. They are so afraid of a false decision that they make none. They spend nights praying for what is already theirs in Christ. They go into vagaries and extremes of "seeking," and sometimes become unbalanced.

There is a happy balance here. All that we need is in Jesus. Let us make no cheap and quick committals until all has been laid at His feet and we really mean business. Long hours of prayer are necessary only if we are stubborn, God is not slow to hear and answer. If we really mean business we need not tarry. Christ is here now, immediately accessible. No use wasting time afraid we are not "sure." We can never be sure of ourselves; He is the sure One!

Walk with God. "Run not before him." Lag not behind Him.

238

## WHERE ARE YOU GOING?

*Lord, to whom shall we go?* JOHN 6:68.

WHERE COULD WE GO? Look down all other roads and see what they have to offer. It is Christ or else. The wisdom of man, the religions of the world, have no answer to the soul's desperate cry, "Where could I go but to the Lord?"

*Where would we go?* If we do not follow the Light we go out into darkness, utter and eternal. We would go to hell if we did not go to Him. "He that believeth not is condemned already."

*Where should we go?* To Jesus of course. Plain common sense tells us that nothing else satisfies. He has proven His case long ago. We ought to be Christians. God commands us to repent and believe.

It is a matter of eternal alternatives: saved or lost, justified or condemned, heaven or hell. "He that is not with me is against me."

"There is a way which seemeth right unto a man." "I am the way." *Which way are you going?*

## IS GOD YOUR FATHER?

*I will be a Father unto you.* II CORINTHIANS 6:18.

YES, IF YOU are born from above by faith in His Son. Popular modern preaching to the contrary notwithstanding, He is the father of them only that believe (Gal. 3:26). Jesus' word to the Pharisees, "Ye are of your father the devil" (John 8:44), is forgotten these days.

But we are told that if we come out and are separate and touch not the unclean thing, God will be a Father unto us.

Does His Fatherhood depend on our separation? No, it depends on our regeneration. But He cannot be to some of us the Father He wants to be because we are not in fellowship. There are fathers who cannot be to their children what they want to be because their children are in no condition for such favors. Sometimes they must be corrected and chastised. What a grief it is to want to do things for a child whose rebellious spirit makes it impossible! God wants to bless us with all the riches of His grace, but He cannot until we are separated from sin and made "blessable."

God may be your Father in relationship and still not be your Father in fellowship. Don't miss anything His Fatherhood holds for you!

<br>

## NOVEMBER 18

### MOVING DAY

*For he that is entered into his rest, he also hath ceased from his own works, as God did from his.* HEBREWS 4:10.

YOU WILL NOT find peace by moving from a big house into a bigger one, by moving from town to country, by moving up the social ladder, by moving from a B.A. to a Ph.D. Moving to the mountains in the summer or south in the winter will not do it. It was an old Negro maid who said of her unhappy globe-trotting mistress, "It don't do her any good, because she has to take herself along!"

But entering into God's rest by simple faith, ceasing from your own works to rest in His finished work, will do it. Do not limit the words, "Entered Into Rest," to a tombstone epitaph. You can enter now.

> Out of my bondage, sorrow and night,
> Jesus, I come; Jesus, I come.

Into Thy freedom, gladness and light,
Jesus, I come to Thee.
Out of my sickness into Thy health;
Out of my want and into Thy wealth;
Out of my sin and into Thyself,
Jesus, I come to Thee.
Moving day!

## NOVEMBER 19

### "TO BE LIKE JESUS"

*For whom he did foreknow, he also did predestinate to
be conformed to the image of his Son.* ROMANS 8:29.

WE MAY NOT understand predestination, and the scholars
may argue about it, but it is very plain what God had in
mind—our conformity to the image of His Son. In other
words, He would have us to be like Jesus. We are all accepted in Him when we believe and are saints as to position, but the working out of all this in our daily lives is
sometimes a slow process. We are stubborn and often "conformed to this world" instead.

It is possible to be a well-instructed fundamentalist who
has progressed in Bible study, attended a lot of meetings,
and learned "all the answers," and yet not be much like
Jesus. Some of us are not much more like Him than we were
ten years ago. We boast that we are not babes but mature
Christians because we can take strong meat in Bible teaching; but are we not still babes if our progress has not been
"in Christ," knowing Him better and becoming more like
Him?

A mature Christian is one who has grown up in Bible
Christlikeness, not merely graduated in Bible courses.

241

## NOVEMBER 20

### "NOTHING WAVERING"

*And shall not doubt in his heart.* MARK 11:23.
*Doubting nothing.* ACTS 10:20.
*But let him ask in faith, nothing wavering.* JAMES 1:6.

IT IS A powerful phrase, and the word shows up elsewhere (Mt. 21:21; Rom. 4:20; 14:23). A. T. Robertson says, "It is a vivid picture of internal doubt."

We must not only believe God, we must believe we believe God. Like the silly habit of going back to see whether you really did lock that door, an unsettled state of spiritual indecision is developed by doubting souls. They never "close the gate" behind them, they are forever reconsidering their decisions. They are never sure of their conversion or their consecration. They are ever learning and never able to come to a knowledge of the truth.

When you have made any covenant with the Lord consider it final. If you did it honestly in the light you had you insult Him and your own intelligence by going over it all again. It becomes a vicious habit, and you can never be sure of anything. You never stand firmly on any point for fear you may be wrong.

Close your gates behind you and move on, "nothing doubting," "for he that wavereth is like a wave of the sea driven with the wind and tossed."

## NOVEMBER 21

### A TROUBLING REMEMBRANCE

*I remembered God, and was troubled.* PSALM 77:3.

ONE WOULD EXPECT it to read, "I remembered God and was comforted." But remembering God may sometimes make us unhappy. As a truant child remembers his parents and dreads their discipline, so when we go astray we remember that evil doing brings consequences. *When we remember God's holiness and our sinfulness we are troubled.*

Then, again, *when we remember God's goodness and our ingratitude we are troubled.* The goodness of God is meant to lead us to repentance. Like the Psalmist here, we call to mind better days and are brought to consider our ways to discover where we have departed from His Way.

Finally, *when we remember God's service and our unfaithfulness we are troubled.* So much to do, so little done! If that does not trouble us, then we are in a low state indeed.

But the kind of trouble the remembrance of God brings is trouble that leads through tears to triumph. May God stir up our minds by way of remembrance, lest we forget Him too long!

### NOVEMBER 22

### RUB IT IN!

*Ye are the salt of the earth.* MATTHEW 5:13.

I HAVE JUST read a statement of a religious leader to the effect that the salt of the earth needs to be rubbed in—even if it smarts.

I have heard and read many developments of the salt theme. The outline usually runs the same course: salt seasons, purifies, preserves. But somebody ought to remind us that salt also irritates. Real living Christianity rubs this world the wrong way. "The world hath hated them, because they are not of the world, even as I am not of the world" (Jno. 1:14). Godly living is in itself a rebuke to this age, and this world resents the light that exposes its corruption.

Billy Sunday used to say, "They tell me I rub the fur the wrong way. I don't. Let the cat turn around."

We are going to a lot of trouble these days developing a brand of Christianity that will not irritate this world. The only salt that will not irritate is "salt without savour," and our Lord said such salt, whether table salt or spiritual salt, is "good for nothing but to be cast out and trodden under foot of men."

## NOVEMBER 23

### PETER'S OTHER CONFESSION

*Then Simon Peter answered him, Lord, to whom shall we go? thou hast words of eternal life. And we believe and are sure that thou art that Christ, the Son of the living God.* JOHN 6:68, 69.

PETER'S CONFESSION IN Matthew 16 is familiar, but this other confession is equally important. Jesus had preached His crowd away, down to the irreducible minimum, the twelve disciples. He asked them, "Will ye also go away?"

Peter's answer moves through three stages. It is cumulative and rises from a good reason for believing on Christ through a better reason to the climax of conviction. It is first a matter of alternatives: "To whom shall we go?" It is Christ—or else. "What other road could we take?" If Jesus does not have the answer, who does?

Then his words: "Never man spake like this man." He has words of eternal life. They sprout, they germinate, they grow. God speaks when Christ speaks, for Christ is God.

And the glorious climax: "We have come to believe and still believe, we have come to know and still know, that you are the Holy One of God." There is no other way like His. There are no other words like His. There is no other One like Him.

## NOVEMBER 24

### WHAT ARE YOU LOOKING AT?

*Looking unto Jesus.* HEBREWS 12:2.

WE HEAR A lot these days about "looking up," "keeping your chin up," and other exhortations, by which this poor world tries to whistle its way past the graveyard. But the value of the uplook depends on what you are looking at. Looking up avails little if it is only a forced optimism staring at the blue sky.

The Christian looks and lives even as the snake-bitten Israelites were healed by a look at the brazen serpent. "Look unto me, and be ye saved," is God's invitation (Isa. 45:22). Then we live the Christian life, "off-looking unto Jesus" (Heb. 12:2). And we live looking for His return (Lk. 21:28; Heb. 9:28). But the value of faith lies in its object, and our look of faith has meaning only if "we see Jesus."

A lot of our present-day looking up sees nothing, for it is not looking at anything. Any object other than Jesus is only a disappointment. He is the only satisfying object of the soul's gaze. "They looked unto him, and were lightened: *and their faces were not ashamed*" (Ps. 34:5). "Looking up" and "smiling through," with a Micawberish hope that something will happen will never get you through. Fix your eyes on Jesus!

## NOVEMBER 25

### MAKING YOURS YOUR OWN

*How long are ye slack to go to possess the land, which the Lord God of your fathers hath given you?* JOSHUA 18:3.

THE PROMISED LAND was theirs but they had not possessed their possessions. It is not what we have but what we know we have that determines our actual wealth. Many a poor man has had an oil well on his farm and didn't know it. If he found that he did have such a treasure he would lose no time tapping his resources. He would not merely brag, "There is oil on my place." Such boasts would not pay bills. He must possess his possessions.

Yet Christians know what they have, but often get no farther than merely boasting of what is potentially but not experientially theirs. Jesus said, "I will give you rest," but He added, "Take my yoke upon you, and learn of me, and ye shall find rest." God gives us oil wells but He does not pump the oil for us. All things are ours in Christ, but we must make what is ours factually our very own actually.

Appreciating what is yours never makes you rich, but appropriating it will. "The Lord is rich unto all that call upon him."

## NOVEMBER 26

### THE LIBERTY OF THE LORD

*Where the Spirit of the Lord is, there is liberty.*
II CORINTHIANS 3:17.

OF COURSE WE must understand this to mean, "Where the Spirit of the Lord is in control, there is liberty." He indwells every believer, but not every believer has come out into the glorious liberty of the children of God. He is present in the churches, even where two or three gather in Christ's Name, but often He is hindered. He is often resident where He is not president!

But wherever He is recognized and obeyed there is no longer a spirit of bondage. In church history the great revival periods have been the blessed liberations in which the Spirit has loosed all bonds and the church has recovered her early freedom. In local churches, what glorious liberty follows when the Spirit is Lord! Read *How Christ Came To Church* and transformed both A. J. Gordon and his Boston pastorate. And the individual Christian "gets loose" only when he is controlled by the Spirit. "Lord" and "liberty" may seem contradictory, but the free man is a controlled man. He has the liberty *of the Lord.* We have "deliberations" aplenty these days, but what we need is liberation!

## NOVEMBER 27

### PREPARED PLACES FOR PREPARED PEOPLE

*I go to prepare a place for you.* JOHN 14:2.
*Be ye also ready.* MATTHEW 24:44.

EVEN IN THIS present world there is always "room at the top," and the man who prepares himself will find a place prepared. There are never enough to go around and there are vacancies always for the man who can really do the job.

In the service of God the harvest is plenteous but the laborers are few, and the eyes of the Lord run to and fro looking for a man with a heart perfect toward Him. Samuel prepared himself and God made ready for Samuel. There is a place ready for you if you are ready for the place.

And there is a place hereafter for those who make ready. There is an inheritance incorruptible, undefiled and that fadeth not away, *reserved in heaven.* But it is reserved for those who are kept by the power of God through faith unto salvation. God not only prepares the place, He prepares His people for the place.

"Lord, prepare me for what Thou art preparing for me."

## BETWEEN TWO FIRES

*And when they had kindled a fire . . . Peter sat down
among them.* LUKE 22:55.
*As soon as they were come to land, they saw a fire of
coals there.* JOHN 21:9.

PETER WARMED HIMSELF at the enemy's fire—and denied
His Lord. The devil always has a convenient fire for saints
who are about to slip. Taking it easy is often the prelude to
backsliding. Comfort precedes collapse.

Days later, Peter warmed at another fire, the coals His
Master had kindled on the beach. There he met the ques-
tion, "Lovest thou me?" and received the commission,
"Feed my sheep."

Many Christians are living in an interim between Satan's
Fire and the Saviour's Fire. If you have fallen because you
warmed yourself when you should have warned yourself,
the Lord seeks an interview. Peter, the backslider, was
marked Special: "Go tell his disciples *and Peter* (Mk. 16:7).
He does not want to fire you out but to fire you up!

If you have collapsed at Satan's Fire, you may be converted at the Saviour's Fire. Do not live "between fires."

## NOVEMBER 29

### SIFTING AND STRENGTHENING

*And the Lord said, Simon, Simon, behold, Satan hath
desired to have you, that he may sift you as wheat: but
I have prayed for thee, that thy faith fail not: and when
thou art converted, strengthen thy brethren.* LUKE 22:
31, 32.

HERE WE HAVE the Triangle of Spiritual Conflict: "Satan—
you—I." Satan would sift us, but we have an Advocate. The

devil asked God for permission to try Job. Here it is Simon Peter he puts through the sifter. And never have more saints been in his hands than today. But he can go only so far. There is one praying for us who defeated Satan, who came to destroy the works of the devil. The Adversary is not in the first two chapters of the Bible, nor is he in the last two. Thank God for a Book that ends with the devil out of business!

But he is very much in business now in the mighty tug-of-war for the souls of men. It is Christ or Antichrist and we are the prize. Peter's faith was eclipsed but not extinct. And when he was converted, he certainly strengthened the brethren and fed the sheep—and does so to this day.

Sometimes we must go through the Sifter before we are of much use for Strengthening.

<br>

### NOVEMBER 30

### "WHERE IT LISTETH"

*The wind bloweth where it listeth.* JOHN 3:8.

WHY IS PREACHING a delight one day, while the next day the chariot wheels drag heavily? Why does the same sermon bring amens one time and yawns the next? Why does one man in church see the heavenly vision, while the one beside him is bored to death? Why does the revival lightning strike there instead of here, then instead of now?

There are many factors, but add them all, and still you are left with an X if you leave this out: "The wind bloweth where it listeth." The Spirit is sovereign to do as He wills. He is not capricious nor does He ignore other factors, but He has the last word.

His movements cannot be charted. Jesus said we cannot determine the whence and where of the wind.

But we can put up our wind mills and be ready!

## DECEMBER 1

### THE GUEST WHO WOULD GO ON

*He made as though he would have gone further.* LUKE
24:28.

OUR LORD DID not force Himself upon the Emmaus disciples. He would have passed on, but He longed to manifest Himself to them and must have been delighted when they constrained Him to tarry.

Have we not sometimes, in the company of one beloved, moved as though we would be going but inwardly hoped we would be asked to remain?

Jesus is passing by. He is a gentleman. He will not abide with us uninvited. If we are to know Him better we must constrain Him. The deeper things of God pass on if we do not lay hold on them. Jesus always makes as though He would go further.

Yet He longs to abide as our Guest, that He may become our Host as He became the Host here and at Cana of Galilee. He sits down at our table, but soon we sit at His. He will sup with us, that we may sup with Him.


## DECEMBER 2

### THE IMPOSSIBLE SYMPHONY

*What concord hath Christ with Belial?* II CORINTHIANS
6:15.

WHAT WE READ as "concord" is really the word from which we get "symphony." "Belial" is found only here in the New Testament, but throughout the Old Testament it stands for the spirit of evil. The spirit of Belial shows up in false religious movements (Dt. 13:13), in lawlessness (Judges 19: 22), in wayward daughters and sons (I Sam. 1:16; 2:12).

250

We have concord with Belial when we oppose God's chosen man (I Sam. 10:27; II Sam. 20:1), when we are sour and churlish (I Sam. 25:17, 25), when we are ungracious toward the weak (I Sam. 30:22), when we bear false witness (I Kgs. 21:10, 13).

There is no "symphony" of Christ with Belial. When we try to harmonize them we have not concord but discord. To be a friend of the world is to be the enemy of God (Jas. 4: 4), and if we love the world, the love of the Father is not in us (I Jno. 2:15).

We are not to effect a truce between Christ and Belial. We are out to issue an ultimatum: "Choose ye this day whom ye will serve."

It is never Christ *and.* It is always Christ *or.* "He that is not with me is against me."

## DECEMBER 3

### "WHAT MORE CAN HE SAY?"

*If they hear not Moses and the prophets, neither will they be persuaded, though one rose from the dead.*
LUKE 16:31.

GOD HAS SPOKEN and that is sufficient. If we cannot depend on His Word, we would not be convinced by any work. Jesus rose from the dead, and still the unbelievers were not persuaded. "He hath said," and if God's Word is not enough, nothing else would ever be enough.

Thomas demanded visible evidence and thereby asked for a lesser blessing than he already had—the joy of believing without seeing. "Blessed are ye that have not seen *and yet* have believed." "In whom, though now ye see him not *yet believing,* ye rejoice with joy unspeakable and full of glory." *Yet believing*—that is it— believing, anyhow!

251

Faith is just taking God at His Word. He will abundantly prove what He has promised, but not until we stand on the promise alone. "Let God be true but every man a liar."

> *What more can He say*
> Than to you He hath said,
> To you who for refuge
> To Jesus have fled?

## DECEMBER 4

### SON IN THE GOSPEL

*Timothy, my own son in the faith.* I TIMOTHY 1:2.

BLESSED IS THE preacher who has a preacher son. But if one has no son in the flesh he may, like Paul, have a son in the faith.

To win a boy to Jesus, like Andrew, to find "a lad here," with his loaves and fishes, and bring him to the Saviour— that is to have a son in the Gospel. Or to show some youth the Heavenly Vision and awaken him to the challenge of the Cross—that is to be a father in the faith.

We are married to Christ, that we should bring forth fruit unto God (Rom. 7:4). Paul speaks of Onesimus as "begotten in my bonds" and of the Corinthians as "begotten through the gospel." He writes to the Galatians, "My little children, of whom I travail in birth again until Christ be formed in you" (Gal. 4:19).

And think of the spiritual grandchildren! The man who led Moody to Christ started a family without number.

How many "children" can you report to the Heavenly Census Taker?

## DECEMBER 5

### "SOME THROUGH THE FIRE"

*And I will bring the third part through the fire.* ZECHA-
RIAH 13:9.

WHY SOME LIVES move along in story-book fashion to happy
endings, while others are a long tale of woe—that is one of
the puzzles we shall have to let eternity explain. We know
only that, while some pilgrims seem to travel mostly in green
pastures and beside still waters, others must know flood and
fire.

"God leads His dear children along," but while they arrive eventually at the same destination, they do not fare the
same en route. We are often perplexed but we need not be
in despair, for even though the furnace be heated seven
times hotter there will be with us one "like the Son of God."

If you seem to have been "chosen in the furnace of affliction," "think it not strange concerning the fiery trial that
is to try you as though some strange thing happened unto
you, but rejoice," because it brands you as a partaker of
Christ's sufferings.

The Great Refiner is at work, and His "refined people"
do not get that way along flowery fields but in fiery furnaces.

## DECEMBER 6

### WHAT'S IN A SURNAME?

*And Simon he surnamed Peter.* MARK 3:16.

OUR LORD HAD two outstanding apostles, Peter and Paul.
Peter He surnamed and Paul He renamed. To Peter He said,
"Thou art Simon . . . thou shalt be called Cephas." A lot
had to happen before the handful of sand become a rock.
But Jesus saw not merely the man he was but the man he

was to be. Not that our Lord went around "seeing the good in everybody," the latent possibilities, calling out "hidden powers." "He knew what was in man." He saw within Simon nothing that Simon could make of himself, but rather what God would make of him.

To educate the old Adam is to make him doubly dangerous. To polish him is to render him far more deceptive. To make him more religious is to leave him tenfold more the child of hell. When Jesus saw Simon, he saw Peter, not by reformation but by transformation.

"Thou art . . . thou shalt be." Move out of your name into your surname! Come to Him just as you are, and by His grace be what you may become! What's in a surname? Everything, when it means that! "And Simon he surnamed Peter."

## DECEMBER 7

### "I'M A STRANGER HERE"

*Dearly beloved, I beseech you as strangers and pilgrims, abstain from fleshly lusts, which war against the soul.* I PETER 2:11.

A STRANGER DOES not feel at home where he is, and neither does a Christian in this world. He is not a citizen of earth trying to get to heaven but a citizen of heaven sojourning on earth. This world is "his passage, not his portion."

We of the Heavenly Commonwealth do not feel at home here, we just "don't belong." We speak another language. When the cocktails are offered we refuse and when the dirty jokes are told we do not join in the laughter, not because of a Pharasaic self-righteousness but simply because we are "strangers." It is not always comfortable to be a "foreigner." And they will think it strange if we don't "make

254

ourselves at home" (I Pt. 4:4), especially if we once took part with them.

The world will do its utmost to make us "one of the crowd." Nothing is more insidious than the hospitality of this age. But, while we need not be discourteous, we must not be deceived.

## DECEMBER 8

### ON PLANNING YOUR PENIEL

*And Jacob was left alone and there wrestled a man with him until the breaking of the day.* GENESIS 32:24.

IT IS NOT in some favored vacation spot, where the setting seems perfect, that we have our best season with the Lord. We do not find our Bethels where we recharge our spiritual batteries in some ideal retreat. It was in desperate loneliness at Jabbok that Jacob met the Lord and gained power with God and men. At the backside of the desert Moses came to the mountain of God. It was in the year that King Uzziah died that Isaiah saw the Lord. Do not forget that John wrote Revelation on Patmos, that *Pilgrim's Progress* came from Bedford jail, and precious hymns from Fanny Crosby's blindness.

Our choicest art and literature came out of poverty and suffering, and God does His best work with us oftimes when it seems that the time and place are most unpropitious. We do not come to know the deeper things by rocking on the porch of some lazy rest spot, sipping lemonade, reading a novel.

You cannot set the stage and arrange the scenery and then work up the experience you need—have it made to order. The Spirit does not work that way. "The wind bloweth where it listeth." It may be in the unlikeliest place and on the darkest day when you are "left alone" that God will come down to wrestle until daybreak.

## DECEMBER 9

### PRESS THROUGH TO JESUS!

*Bring him hither to me.* MATTHEW 17:17.

THE DISCIPLES HAD failed to cast out demons from this poor boy, but Jesus never fails. How good to know that when men fail and churches fail, we can still get through to Jesus. Back of all the fads and isms, the failures of the saints and the impotency of some churches, He stands, the same yesterday *and today* and forever.

You will find what you need in Jesus. Not in that book which you hope will reveal some magic open sesame on the next page. Not in some group or denomination that seems to have just what you've been looking for. Not in some self-induced experience you've been trying to work up. Not in a pet preacher or favorite cause or doctrine. All these will disappoint you. Our Lord said of the hungry multitude, "They need not depart." You never need to leave Jesus for anything. He is Alpha and Omega—and all the letters between—so you need not go outside His alphabet to complete the wording of your life.

All that is true in any book or movement or group or doctrine or experience is already in Christ. Get through to the Source. "By him all things consist."


## DECEMBER 10

### NOT LOST IN THE CROWD

*Thou seest the multitude thronging thee, and sayest thou, Who touched me?* MARK 5:31.

GOD NEVER LOSES the individual in the crowd. "All have sinned and come short of the glory of God"—there is the multitude—but God breaks it down into individuals—"there is none righteous, no, not *one.*" The sinners cannot hide in the crowd.

But there is another side: "God so loved the world"—there is the multitude—"that He gave his only begotten Son, that whosoever"—there is the individual—"believeth on him should not perish but have everlasting life." Salvation is for every sinner in the crowd.

The disciples in our text saw the crowd; Jesus saw one lone woman. The multitude *thronged* Him; the woman *touched* Him. The crowds at church on Sunday morning *throng* Him, but few ever *touch* Him. God deals with people one at a time. "*Him* that cometh . . . If any man . . . Whosoever will" We are saved, Spirit-filled, called, directed, one at a time.

Be sure you press through the throng and *touch* Him. "For as many as *touched* [not *thronged*] him were made perfectly whole."

### DECEMBER 11

### NAZARETH OR CANA?

*And he did not many mighty works there because of their unbelief.* MATTHEW 13:58.

HERE WE HAVE the *Person* ("He"), the *Place* ("there"), and the *People* ("their"). Jesus, the Person, was in Nazareth, the Place. It could have been a place of blessing but for the People. "Where"—there is the *place*—"two or three are gathered in my name"—there are the *People*—"there am I in the midst of them"—there is the *Person.*

If revival does not come to your church, it will be because of the unbelief of the people. We can limit the Holy One of Israel. We can grieve and quench the Holy Spirit.

257

Jesus had a better reception in Cana. Whatsoever He said, they did it, and water became wine. The ruler of the feast did not understand, but the servants who drew the water knew. God's secrets are hid from the wise and prudent but revealed unto babes. Christ works His miracle when humble servants fill the waterpots with water. Faith and obedience change the mediocre to the miraculous.

Do you live in Nazareth or Cana?


## DECEMBER 12

## BOUNDARIES OF BLESSING

*According to your faith be it unto you.* MATTHEW 9:29.

YOU CAN BELIEVE God too little but not too much. That does not mean that He will honor faith for some unwise extravagant thing outside the circle of your need and His will. But there is room for plenty of miracles within His will. You won't feel cramped!

"Believe *ye* that I am able to do *this?*" There are three angles to this matter: "YE," "I," "THIS." Our faith, His power, our need. The boundaries of His blessing are "according to his will," "according to your faith," "all your need."

But do not think "all your need" means something like "bare necessities." He gives liberally and upbraids not, gives more than we can ask or think, all sufficiency in all things, abundance of grace. He is plenteous in mercy. All things are ours.

Within His wide horizons you can never ask too much. If without faith it is impossible to please Him, then great faith must please Him much.

## IS YOUR EXPERIENCE AUTHENTIC?

*And the men which journeyed with him stood speech-
less, hearing a voice, but seeing no man.
And they that were with me saw indeed the light, and
were afraid.* ACTS 9:7; 22:9.

PAUL'S COMPANIONS HAD an "experience," but they did not
meet the Lord. It is possible to be present when great
things happen without great things happening to you. It
would have made a great story to tell afterwards about
seeing a light, being afraid, hearing a voice, and standing
speechless. That is about all that some witnesses are able
to relate. One of Job's comforters, Eliphaz, had quite a hair-
raising account to give, but he knew little of God.

It was Paul who got through to Christ: "Who art thou,
Lord? . . . Lord, what wilt thou have me to do?" The im-
portant thing is to hear the Word of God and keep it, as
Jesus said to the woman who spoke out in the meeting.

It is not enough to jump up and tell about seeing a light
and hearing a voice. Did you face up to the "Who" and
"What"—who the Lord is and what He wants you to do?
There will be variations as to the lights you see and the
voices you hear, but the "Who" and "What" are standard,
they make the authentic experience.

## DECEMBER 14

### SERPENTS AND DOVES

*Behold, I send you forth as sheep in the midst of
wolves: be ye therefore wise as serpents, and harmless
as doves.* MATTHEW 10:16.

SERPENTS AND DOVES! What two creatures could be more
unlike? Yet there are characteristics of each which a Chris-

tian should have. For the lack of either he may suffer greatly and cause others to suffer.

We must be wise, keen, alert, not ignorant of Satan's devices, trying the spirits, proving all things and holding fast that which is good. We are not to be stupid, gullible, carried about with every wind of doctrine. We need plenty of sanctified common sense, discernment, sagacity. We are to walk not as fools but as wise.

But we can become critical, coldly analytical, professional, proud of our wisdom, and fail to be blameless and harmless, the sons of God without rebuke. Our serpent sagacity must be coupled with a dovelike gentleness, else we become hard-boiled when we are only half-baked.

To be wise and yet winsome, staying simple and plain and old-fashioned and wholesome, is an attainment wrought by the Spirit. It is the exact opposite of this sophisticated age. It is the mark of a well-developed Christian.

## DECEMBER 15

### JUST FAITHFUL

*It is required in stewards, that a man be found faithful.*
I CORINTHIANS 4:2.

IT IS NOT given to all Christians to witness a spectacular work of God either in their own spiritual experience or in their ministry. That is no indication of Divine disapproval. The Spirit divideth severally as He will, and to some are given special manifestations in His sovereign purpose for special reasons.

We are prone to measure our experience in the light of some colorful testimony, and grow depressed because we saw no vision or heard no voice. Or, compared with the sensational demonstration in the ministry of another, our little work may look drab and uneventful. It is well to remember just here that Matthew Henry considered his pastoral work almost a failure, but his commentary stands on the shelves of thousands of preachers' studies today.

To be sure, we may be living short of what God has for us. But if we are in His will as best we know, it is required only that we be faithful. Promotion hereafter is for being faithful now, "faithful over a few things," "faithful in that which is least."

<br>

## DECEMBER 16

### SAINTS OF THE GOURD VINE

*Thou hast had pity on the gourd . . . and should not I spare Nineveh, that great city?* JONAH 4:10, 11.

JONAH WAS WORRIED about a gourd but not concerned about Nineveh. Too many of us are more occupied with the gourd vines of our own comfort than burdened over the need of a world. Then, too, Nineveh's repentance made Jonah appear mistaken in his prophecy of doom. It may be that some prophets today may almost seem disappointed if men repent when they expected ruin instead. A turning to God among sinners today would make some Jonahs peevish, for their programs did not anticipate an upset.

Beware of getting wrought up over a gourd, more interested in sitting in the shade than in rejoicing over the salvation of souls. And how a complacent fundamentalism needs to get out from under its arbors and trellises, losing its life to find it in evangelizing a lost world!

<br>

## DECEMBER 17

### HAVE YOU BEEN "MAGNETIZED"?

*Ye shall receive power . . . ye shall be witnesses unto me.* ACTS 1:8.

ONE OF THE wonders of my boyhood days was the first little horseshoe magnet I ever saw. How I marveled at the way

it could lift a nail and then, more marvelous still, enable
that nail to lift another! It seemed to give power to other
objects and yet lose none of its own.

A friend of mine had a knife that had this strange power
to lift other objects. He explained: "It has been in touch
with a magnet—it is magnetized."

I have seen men and women who years ago met Jesus
Christ. He gave them of His power without losing any of
His own. Now they touch others and there is something
that nothing earthly can explain. As they live in touch with
Him they touch others, and these others touch still others,
and on it goes through the years and around the world, the
chain magnetism of power committed and transmitted.

Think of the man who led Moody to Christ. How that
empowered life touched its generation and how those who
touched Moody touched others, and the process goes on
still. Grenfell of the Labrador was touched, and that "nail"
picked up many another. And Grenfell was only one of
thousands.

"Ye shall receive power . . . ye shall be [my] witnesses."
This world has its tricks of personal magnetism, but God's
plan is Christ drawing us and, through us, others.

## DECEMBER 18

### GOD UNDERSTANDS

*But thou, O Lord, knowest me.* Jeremiah 12:3.

God knows our downsitting and uprising, He understands
our thought afar off. He compasses our path and our lying
down, and is acquainted with all our ways" (Ps. 139:2, 3).

"Nobody understands me." Well, you are no exception.
Does anybody really understand anybody else? We do not
understand our own selves. How often have we done things
and wondered afterward what made us do them!

Paul said (I Cor. 4:3–5) that neither he nor others were

capable of judging his ministry. Only God is competent. "Therefore judge nothing before the time, until the Lord come." While we are to judge sin in our lives (I Cor. 11:31), we cannot size up ourselves or others properly. We may put our estimate too high or too low. God knows all the facts, and He will give the correct measure of praise or blame.

Do not unduly boast or belittle. You do not know the hidden motives, the complicated tangle of your own self or anyone else. But He knows. So wait patiently for that day, and let God make His appraisal.

## DECEMBER 19

### "IT IS FINISHED"

*It is finished.* JOHN 19:30.

PRECIOUS WORDS THAT released young Hudson Taylor from years of doubt and striving! While reading a tract his eyes caught the words, "The finished work of Christ." He had known for years of the atoning work of Christ, but for the first time he saw that if it were a finished work there was nothing for him to do but accept it and praise God forever.

*God has taken care of everything in Christ.* My sins, my salvation, my life, my past and present and future, all my needs and the needs of the whole world, are all wrapped up in a finished work. If God has taken care of everything I do not need to try to take care of anything. I have only to believe, receive, rejoice, and then out of the fulness of my heart love and obey Him.

No matter what comes up, there is provision for it in Christ. And when we find that everything is in Jesus, He becomes to us everything!

"Finished"—not something with ragged edges and frazzled ends that I must piece out. God has taken care of everything forever in Christ. And we are complete in Him.

## DECEMBER 20

### "THE SEEMING VOID"

*Faith is . . . the evidence of things not seen.* HEBREWS
11:1.

> Nothing before, nothing behind,
> The steps of faith
> Fall on *the seeming void*
> And find the rock beneath.

How OFTEN HAVE we seemed to "step out on nothing," to find underneath the Everlasting Arms. Well, God hangs the earth on nothing (Job 26:7), and surely He will sustain us on what seems a void.

"The Rock beneath" is Christ, "whom having not seen" we love, and in whom, though now we see Him not, we rejoice with joy unspeakable and full of glory. We cannot see Him now, and yet by faith we do see Jesus (Heb. 2:9). What seems a void is oft the darkness that veils His lovely face, but faith rests on His unchanging grace.

How is it that "though now we see him not" we can still say, "But we see Jesus"? The answer is in two little words we left out above on purpose—"yet believing." Faith walks out on the seeming void in the assurance of the Rock beneath. We have God's Word for it. Stand on the Verse while you step on the Void!

### DECEMBER 21

### CAGED CHRISTIANS

*They that wait upon the Lord shall . . . mount up with wings as eagles.* ISAIAH 40:31.

IN A SMALL ZOO I watched a caged hawk vainly fan its wings as it longingly sought to break out of its prison and soar in the limitless sky. It was not made nor meant for the narrow confines of those bars. Again and again I have seen souls caged by sin beating against the walls with which Satan has hedged them in. They were meant for higher things!

Alas, how many "snared saints" become "Christians in a coop"! Evil habits, circumstances, more things than stone walls and iron bars, make prisons and cages. We are made for "high living"—God's "high life," of which this poor world knows nothing.

If Satan has cooped you, fly your coop! God made you for an eagle, and eagles are not made for cages. They are meant for high altitudes and lofty peaks. There is plenty of room for "high flying" in the life that is hid with Christ in God.

Do not confuse "flying the coop" with a mere change of conditions. Circumstances, health may improve, but the soul be still in bondage. Paul's body was in bonds, but his spirit was free in the liberty of Christ. He was a "prisoner of Jesus Christ." When He makes us His captive He sets us free.

### DECEMBER 22

### THE PARLEY AND THE PERSON

*Why reason ye among yourselves?* MATTHEW 16:8.

I HAVE HEARD recently of a group of Christians from different churches who began to meet periodically to discuss various problems which had arisen. But the more they met and the more they discussed, the bigger their problems grew. Finally, someone suggested, "Why don't we forget about our problems for a while and gather just to talk about Christ?" So they began to come together to consider Jesus, to sit at His feet and learn of Him through His Word. And, lo, their problems began to dissolve as they fell in love afresh with Him and with each other.

A good revival would dispose of most of our committee meetings on how to do what. He stands amidst our feverish get-togethers, whether small board meetings or vast conventions, and asks, "Why reason ye among yourselves because ye have no bread?" A genuine heart-warming in His Presence is the surest and quickest way to clear the agenda. The way out is not by a parley but by a Person.

## DECEMBER 23

### GOD AS A GARDENER

*Supposing him to be the gardener.* JOHN 20:15.

MEN HAVE SOMETIMES mistaken the voice of "gardeners" for the voice of God, but then, again, it is easy to mistake God for the gardener. Remember that day in our Lord's ministry when the Father spoke from heaven and some said, "It thundered"?

Our Lord does not always manifest Himself with His first word. Sometimes He speaks to ask the simplest question. "Woman, why weepest thou?" Anyone could have asked that. But He is interested in our griefs and sorrows.

And then He may want to lead us out by His simple inquiry. Think of how He asked Philip concerning the hungry multitude: "Whence shall we buy bread, that these may eat?"

God does not always break on us with the glory of Isaiah's vision or Paul's blinding light on the Damascus road. Sometimes He appears in a manner so plain that we suppose Him to be the gardener.

Do not ignore His lowliest approach. Tell Him your trouble, and the next word, as here, may bring the needed revelation.

## STAND UP AND BE COUNTED!

*And the people answered him not a word.* I KINGS
18:21.

THERE WERE SEVEN thousand in Israel who had not bowed
their knees to Baal. There were four hundred and fifty
prophets of Baal. They could be counted, but Elijah's
audience was noncommittal. They did not declare themselves. They were spectators, onlookers.

Too many Christians are in the grandstand when they
should be on the team. Too many are snug at home reading
communiques from the front instead of going to the battle.

Too many in our meetings are spectators. They are great
onlookers. They get used to it at the movies and in the
stadium, and they come to church to be entertained.

But we are all participants in eternal issues, whether we
know it or not. "He that is not with me is against me, and
he that gathereth not with me scattereth abroad." We cannot play hands off and answer not a word.

"The Lord knoweth them that are his," but He wants us
to stand up and be counted.


## DECEMBER 25

### GOD SENT HIS SON

*Last of all he sent unto them his Son.* MATTHEW 21:37.

IN ALL THE confusion and commercialization of Christmas
these days we are more than likely to lose Christ. Let us
never forget that God sent not merely a prophet, a philoso-
pher, a leader, to meet the world's need. He gave His only
begotten Son (Jno. 3:16). Like the man in the parable, He
said, "I will send my beloved Son" (Lk. 20:13). He spared
not His own Son (Rom. 8:32).

A little boy accustomed to seeing service stars in windows during the war exclaimed as he watched the evening star at sunset, "God must have a son in the war!" The story has been misapplied, but in the age-old struggle with sin God truly gave His Son.

Remember at Christmas that the Gospel is not that Jesus came or that He lived or that He taught. He could have done all that, but if He had returned to the Father some other way than by Calvary and the open tomb, we would still be in our sins.

Thank God He was born. But He was born to die and live again, that we might live forever.

## DECEMBER 26

### ARE YOU LISTENING

*Speak; for thy servant heareth.* I SAMUEL 3:10.
*He that hath ears to hear, let him hear.* MATTHEW 11:15.
*He that hath an ear, let him hear.* REVELATION 2:7.

IT IS AN oft-recurring word from our Lord, found throughout the Gospels—"He that hath ears to hear . . ." Some have ears—period! Samuel was listening—and God spoke. God has much to say today, but we have "ears to hear, and hear not" (Ezek. 12:2). Some stop their ears (Acts 7:57). Some turn their ears from the truth (II Tim. 4:4). Some have itching ears (II Tim. 4:3).

Are you tuned in on God? It is said that John Burroughs, the naturalist, could walk along a noisy street and overhear a cricket in the hedge. His ear was tuned to the little voices of nature. You can make your way through the hubbub and still keep in touch with heaven.

Samuel was listening. The boy who listens for God to speak will hear Him, for God is looking for such boys. God's men have been men of a double resolve: "I will hear what God the Lord will speak" (Ps. 85:8); and then, "What the Lord saith unto me, that will I speak" (I Kgs. 22:14).

## DECEMBER 27

### DO YOU MEAN BUSINESS?

*The night following the Lord stood by him, and said, Be of good cheer, Paul.* ACTS 23:11.

SOME THINK PAUL should not have gone up to Jerusalem on this visit. Some think he should not have taken a vow as he was advised to do. Still others think that his behavior on trial compares poorly with that of our Lord.

Be all that as it may, the Lord knew Paul's heart and so stood by him to cheer him up and to assure him that he would witness also in Rome.

God does not measure us by isolated incidents. Man looks on the outward appearance, but the Lord looks on the heart. A good man may blunder and fall far below the standard, but God looks at the real motive, the general purpose of the heart. Some may do exceedingly well at times whose true heart is undependable. Others may fail at times, but their inmost self is right with God.

God knew that Paul meant business, and that is what counts with Him. He does business with those who mean business.

## DECEMBER 28

### NOT COPIES BUT CHILDREN

*The pattern shewed to thee in the mount.* HEBREWS 8:5.

THERE IS ALWAYS such a wide gulf between the ideal and the actual. The best we are and do looks so little like the

Perfect Example, like a little child's scrawl below the model line. But we can be blameless, though not faultless (Phil. 2:15).

Sometimes we expect too much. We break ourselves with demands on ourselves that God never made. He knows our frame and remembers that we are dust. He remembers what we so often forget, and, as another has said, forgets what we remember—our sins!

But we can also expect too little and be content to plod when we ought to fly. We are to be perfect as He is, perfect with a perfection which He both demands and supplies.

It is not imitation, however, but identification—"Christ liveth in me." Christians are not mimics trying to copy Christ in their feeble strength. They are children of God in whom Christ lives again.

## DECEMBER 29

### BACK TO THE SPRING

*The simplicity that is in Christ.* II CORINTHIANS 11:3.

SAID A. J. GORDON: "Would that our teachers of theology were content to know less that they might know more, that they were less endued with the spirit of modern thought and more deeply baptized by that Spirit that has been sent to us that we might know the things that are freely given to us of God."

We sadly need to be converted and become as little children. We know too much. We have read and heard everything. The happiest person is a young Christian before he has met too many Bible scholars! We need more than anything else some plain and simple Christians who will let God be true and every man a liar.

We have read of a spring whose medicinal waters became famous, so that eventually a city grew around it. But there came a time when in the rush of progress the spring was lost and finally could not be located.

We have built around the Spring until we have lost it. Blessed are they who rediscover the simplicity that is in Christ!

## DECEMBER 30

### ONLOOKER OR FORTHTELLER?

*Ye shall be witnesses.* ACTS 1:8.

"WHAT BEGAN AS a company of lay witnesses has become a professional pulpitism financed by lay spectators." While some are especially called to be preachers, all are appointed to be witnesses. Alas, we are too often witnesses in the sense of onlookers! Every believer in the Early Church was a missionary. They were all advertising the Gospel.

Something was happening every minute. Some were expelled, like Ananias and Sapphira. Some were repelled—"And of the rest durst no man join himself to them." But the real believers were compelled—"We cannot but speak the things which we have seen and heard."

The Gospel spreads when the church ceases to be a sanctified club sedately listening to the minister as though he were paid to do all the witnessing for all of them and when it begins to be a company of lay evangelists testifying to small and great the wonderful works of God.

Which kind of witness are you, an onlooker or a forthteller?

## DECEMBER 31

### JOURNEY'S END

*That I might finish my course with joy.* ACTS 20:24.

PAUL WAS GRANTED his heart's desire. "I have finished my course," he wrote later, and it was with joy. Not with

271

money or earthly possessions, because he wrote from a dark dungeon, needing his cloak and parchments. Not with a host of friends, for all men forsook him. Not with fame, for he died a martyr. But he finished with joy, anticipating a crown.

Just as the last day of the year anticipates a new year, so Journey's End for the Christian is but the end of a Prelude. "To depart and be with Christ is far better." There are no "turns for the worse." "To die is gain," so even death is a paying proposition.

It was *for the joy that was set before him* that our Lord endured the cross, despising the shame. And looking unto Him we run with patience and finish with joy.

Some who have known starting grace and sustaining grace have grown careless about finishing grace. What fools we can be on the last mile! Be sure to make your last testimony the Joy of Journey's End!